The Calm and The Strife

IN SEARCH OF LIFE'S SPIRITUAL MESSAGE FROM THE O.J. SIMPSON TRIALS

BY JOHN AND ALICE JOHNSON, Ed.D.
Authors of *Mysterious Stranger Aboard*, *Love Paints Beauty in the Soul* and *Let Your Attitude Be Gratitude*

With a Foreword by
Detective Therese Homer, Executive Director
Domestic Violence Interventions of FL, Inc.

Published by MAL-JONAL PRODUCTIONS, INC., MIAMI, FL

Mal-Jonal Productions, Inc. 16713 SW 107 Place
Miami, FL 33157-2965

Printed in the United States of America
Cover Design by ***Creative**Color*

Library of Congress Catalog Card Number: 97-71784
Johnson, John and Alice
The Calm and the Strife
ISBN 0-9648271-2-3

Affectionately dedicated to our beloved parents, the late Annie and Abraham Lincoln Ward and the late Mary Louise and John Johnson, Sr., who showed us that love finds expression through kindness and concern.

About The Story

Moved by the O.J. Simpson "Trial of the Century" and how the trials have brought racism and domestic violence to the forefront, John and Alice Johnson, in *The Calm and The Strife*, have written another nonfiction fast-paced, page turner. The book depicts racism and domestic violence based on life experiences. The Johnsons show how this behavior shatters the continuity of the family, destroys healthy relationships, individuals and spirituality.

They speak of the predominately Black criminal trial jurors who found Simpson not guilty for the murders of his wife, Nicole Brown Simpson, and her friend, Ron Goldman, on the night of June 12, 1994; and the predominately White civil trial jurors who found Simpson liable for the murders. They speak of how African Americans and Whites responded to the verdicts, and how the masses were sent a most disturbing message that justice is in the color of the beholder. Alice and John speak of how the trials awakened Whites and Blacks to our world that is sometimes divided and hostile.

Feeling depressed by this disturbing message, the Johnsons revisit the Book of *Genesis* to focus on crime and human nature. They discover that the book addresses in a very urgent way, root problems of our existence as individuals, as families and as a nation. They discover that *Genesis*, like the Simpson case, is like a soap opera in that *Genesis* starts with the creation of the world, then hurries on toward Adam and Eve's temptation and fall, the murder of Abel and his brother, Cain, in which the ego which is capable of viciousness at worst, projects our inherited selfishness; and the story of Noah; then there is Abraham and Sarah's fertility problem and the attendant strife this causes; there is Sodom and Gomorrah; and at the end of *Genesis*, there is Joseph's abandonment by his brothers and then the forgiveness that heals family wounds, exemplifying that love finds expression through kindness and concern.

The Calm and the Strife reveals that as far back as the beginning of time, some people have always considered themselves dominant over others based on gender, race, color, class or status. Researching *The Holy Bible* and other spiritual books emphasizing that love finds expression through kindness and concern, the Johnsons conclude that the walls of hostility can be broken, and that healing the pain and suffering of racism and violence must be our priority agenda as we, a united people in a multicultural society, continue this spiritual journey on planet earth.

-Larcenia J. Bullard-Florida State Representative

FOREWORD

DOMESTIC VIOLENCE... These are two words which mean so much more than most people will ever know. Oftentimes, people will quickly say: "I know all that I need to know about domestic violence." "It happens to those people." "I will never be involved in a domestic violence situation." "He's not hitting me, it's just verbal." Many believe they know everything there is about domestic violence. They believe that the answer to the violence is to just leave the first time he hits. "The first time that he hits me, I'm outta there!"

If you think that way, if this all rings a bell to you, then you should read this book, *The Calm and the Strife* by John and Alice Johnson, and pass it on to those you know who have the same views. There is never too much anyone can ever know about domestic violence. As a law enforcement officer for twenty years, I am constantly learning new things about domestic violence every day.

DOMESTIC VIOLENCE is a buzz word to let everyone know specifically what the relationship is of the parties involved. This is what the term **"domestic"** is describing: generally, it means husbands and wives, boyfriends and girlfriends, people who live together, people who have a child in common, people related by blood or marriage. **"Violence"** means the type of crime committed. For example, an assault (a verbal threat to do bodily harm); a battery (a hit, a kick, a shove, a pinch, spitting on someone, pulling someone's hair); a burglary, vandalism, and so forth.

In the State of Florida **DOMESTIC VIOLENCE** is defined as "any assault, aggravated assault, battery, aggravated battery, sexual assault, sexual battery, stalking, aggravated stalking, or any criminal offense resulting in physical injury or death by one family or household member by another who is or was residing in the same single dwelling unit. **"Family or household member"** means spouses, former spouses, persons related by blood or marriage, persons who are presently residing together, as if a family, or who have resided together in the past, as if a family, and persons who have a child in common regardless of whether they have been married or have resided together at any time.

As you can see, domestic violence covers any and all crimes. The difference between domestic violence and any other crime is the relationship between perpetrator and victim. In domestic violence incidents, the parties know each other and /or they are generally related by blood or married or are involved in an intimate relationship. In other criminal incidents generally, those involved are strangers or acquaintances and there is no intimacy.

For too long domestic violence crimes have been on the back burner. They have been viewed as "family secrets," private matters between a husband and wife or boyfriend and girlfriend, or whoever is involved. The victims in these incidents are beaten (battered), shot (aggravated assault), cut, run over, held hostages in their own homes, raped and sodomized, set on fire, and otherwise mistreated.

These victims, usually women, oftentimes feel trapped in their own homes and their situations. They feel that there's no way out. They feel helpless and hopeless. They feel like the beatings,and all the other bad times, are all their fault. They have been told that they are stupid, ugly, too fat, too skinny, etc. They've teen told that they can't do anything right. They've been called "bitch," "whore." "gay," "fool," "a—h—," and any other vile name.

In *The Calm and the Strife*, the Johnsons, in their reference, point to the biblical character Cain killing his brother Abel to show that domestic violence has been around for quite a long time.

Society has just recently given it a name, "DOMESTIC VIOLENCE." So, let's stop minimizing what the term domestic violence means. This is a real crime. It just has to be looked at a little differently than all other crimes because of the closeness of the parties involved. A stranger abusing another will most likely not see the other again; but people involved in domestic relationships will continue to see each other and will most likely run into each other. Domestic violence is real, and many, many women and children are dying for love!

Statistics reveal that women continue to be the overwhelming victims of domestic violence. An act of domestic violence occurs every nine seconds in the United States. Nationally, statistics reveal that 95% of victims of domestic violence are women. They report that approximately 5% of victims of domestic violence are men. Statistics also reveal that domestic violence crimes are the most under reported of all crimes even though they are the most common of all crimes. In fact, they are more common than automobile accidents, rapes and muggings combined. According to the last Surgeon General, domestic violence is the number one health risk to women in the United States. It has also been noted that one of the leading causes of birth defects is domestic violence when women are being beaten while pregnant. As a matter of fact, when women get pregnant, the incidents of domestic violence tend to increase. Domestic violence has been noted as one of the primary reasons a woman visits the emergency room of hospitals. Domestic violence affects all races, ethnic groups, religions, cultures and socioeconomic classes. I would like to say that domestic violence is an "equal opportunity crime."

We can not afford to let the flames of the issue die. The Nicole Brown Simpson and Ron Goldman murders brought the issue into the spotlight. Prior to this, many people thought that domestic violence was a poor issue, a Black issue. Now, however, society and the world has been put on notice that "Domestic Violence" is a crime and will no longer be tolerated, and that anybody can be a victim. Let us not let Nicole, Ron and all other victims who have been murdered or who are still trapped in their abusive relationships suffer in vain. We must fight for our children's right to know love——unconditional love and peace. Our children are growing up witnessing this violence (thus learning domestic violence). They will grow up to either be abusers themselves or victims because they're learning subliminal messages that abuse is okay because this is how one is suppose to show love.

We must continue to keep the issue alive and out there. We have to continue to fight to end domestic violence in our society and adopt a "Zero Tolerance" attitude toward it. We can't accept any form of abuse whether physical, emotional/psychological or sexual as a normal way of life. It isn't. We need to be open to learn new ways to attack the epidemic.

The Calm and the Strife: In Search of Life's Spiritual Message from the O. J. Simpson Trials is a new and fresh way of looking at domestic violence. It is filled with personal abuse incidents involving the writer, Alice, who was once a victim of domestic violence herself, and her family, friends and acquaintances. The writers parallel domestic violence today with some domestic violence incidents in the book of *Genesis* in the Bible. In an attempt to understand domestic violence, the authors state that "The book of *Genesis* showed us that man makes his own heaven or hell by his thoughts and feelings." If we think we are victims, we will continue to be victims. On the other hand, if we think we are victors/survivors, we will overcome the situation and become victors.

We all have one thing in common, regardless of race, ethnicity, culture, gender or class. That is, I believe, a belief in a higher power. As a police detective, I have worked intensively for the past six years with domestic violence victims. I have not seen nor read much literature on Spirituality and Domestic Violence. Everyone, including law enforcement, victim advocates, legislators, attorneys, judges, and others who regularly encounter domestic violence issues and situations have been looking for the answers to how do we end domestic violence? Spirituality and Domestic Violence is an avenue which has not been explored very much. Maybe this way will give us another message from the insight of a new spiritual "common sense." John and Alice in *The Calm and the Strife* embrace the universal message: "*Treat others as you would have them treat you.*" In semblance, they embrace the teachings of the Buddha: "*See yourself in others; whom can you harm?*"

The Johnsons have learned from their forty-year experiences of being educators and community leaders that ingratitude is at the root of domestic violence. They feel that our children, early in life, should be taught by example the spiritual message: "Let your attitude be gratitude," and that they should keep a daily journal of experiences for which they are grateful just as TV talk show hostess Oprah Winfrey suggested to her viewers. Adhering to Oprah's suggestion and following through with daily journaling, the Johnsons have learned that it is *not experiences* that give us wisdom, but it is *thinking about experiences* that gives us wisdom. They feel that we can let the healing of our society begin in early childhood so that we, as parents and educators, can help raise a generation of children with high moral and spiritual values and a sense of personal responsibility.

As a dedicated police officer, I am open for suggestions and new insights. How about you? Are you committed to helping your sisters and those trapped in abusive relationships or who, according to the authors, are so much in love with being married that they don't even know that they are being abused? And when they are abused, do they sweep it under the rug and run out of the marriage without trying to fight the violence to save future generations?

John and Alice learned from the Simpson trials that "domestic violence, indeed, shatters the continuity of the family, destroys healthy relationships, destroys individuals and destroys spirituality."

Those of you who have been working to help stop domestic violence know that we've come a long way, baby, but we have a much longer way to go. To those of you who need to join us in this fight, we say to you: Don't give up and don't get tired and tune out when you hear the term "Domestic Violence." Get "angry" in a healthy way, and get motivated like the Johnsons, and find a way to help those victims you know who are locked in their world of domestic abuse amid the calm and the strife.

—Detective Therese Homer, Executive Director,
Domestic Violence Interventions of Florida, Inc.

ACKNOWLEDGMENTS

First and foremost, we want to thank our parents and family members who taught us the joy of loving the Creator and all creation, and the joy of loving others when we were little children unaware of what life is all about. We thank our religious leaders and teachers of all races and nationalities who have continued to lead and teach us that the essence of life is love, and for answering our many questions about life, love, faith, suffering, good and evil.

We thank our media for bringing us the O.J. Simpson trials and for keeping the public informed of life's many experiences, providing us with opportunities to share in these experiences with the understanding that they are geared to help us grow spiritually as a multicultural nation. We especially thank Father Clancy, our priest, who shared with us his philosophy: "Let your attitude be gratitude," and our dear friend, Dr. Rose Watson, for her sincere encouragement and for being our mentor.

We sincerely thank graphic artist John Penney of CreativeColor for his artistic creativeness in designing this book; Janell Walden Agyeman of Marie Brown Associates for literary guidance; and talk show hostess Oprah Winfrey for her insights on attitude/gratitude that gave us the motivation to write this book.

Again, Drs. John and Alice Johnson remind us to look at our circumstances through God's promises with an attitude of gratitude amid the calm and the strife. Thank you, John and Alice, for this timely challenge to teach with your life and to live with disciplined contentment as life's struggles intensify.

- Arthur A. Hayward and the Adult 111
Sunday School Class of Mt. Calvary
Missionary Church, Dayton, Ohio

Great work and a beautiful testimony. Thanks for sharing this book with us!

- Clarence & Greeta Johnson

Revisiting the book of *Genesis*, John and Alice Johnson in *The Calm and the Strife* reveal that ever since the beginning of time, some people have always considered themselves dominant over others based on gender, race, color, class or status. When we see ourselves in others, we are evolving spiritually. Excellent reading.

- Rosie Milligan, Ph.D., Author, *Resource Guide for African-American Speakers and Writers*

This is a great book written from life's first hand experiences to guide us in overcoming and help us grow spiritually. For those who believe there are no answers to our many problems of domestic abuse, even amid the royal circle, *The Calm and the Strife* will change your minds, because we humans are the answers.

- Mary Thompson, Ed.D.
Religious Counselor

CHAPTER ONE

And he said unto them, "Do violence to no man, neither accuse any falsely." Luke 3:14

"Love finds expression through kindness and concern," I tearfully read, editing the epitaph into the unfinished manuscript of Patty's life story which I was documenting, and recalling how violently the beautiful 17-year old playmother died. I was six-years-old and in the first grade at Tomlinson School in Kingstree, South Carolina when Patty McNeil, my beloved playmother, was in the eleventh. The statement, which now pierces my heart, was her eternal epitaph.

I continued to read, my mind traveling vicariously with the story I was writing on racism and domestic violence in search of life's spiritual message from the O.J. Simpson trials. Why? Because the Creator commanded us to love one another. We all need spiritual strength to love one another unconditionally as He loves us. The universal message from the trials seemed beyond comprehension, the synthesis of a new spiritual common sense.

It was January 1997 and two-o'clock in cloudless morning as I sat editing the story into the loneliness of our Miami suburban home... a creepy loneliness that stole the space of my scholarly, beloved husband, John, whom Hurricane Andrew's 1992 angry winds had blown into Miami's Veterans Administration Medical Center Nursing Home. John has severe multiple sclerosis.

Comments of the O. J. Simpson civil trial flowed from our home-based office intercom, projecting my spiritual thoughts and feelings that man is a social being who needs the companionship and affection of other human beings from cradle to grave. And because the case was educational, my mind refused to turn off the facility and stay focused on editing the material. Instead, I turned it up, pensively absorbing comments of Simpson's acquittal on charges he murdered his ex-wife, Nicole Simpson, and her friend Ron Goldman in June 1994, and would the civil trial find him liable, thus , forcing racism and domestic abuse to the forefront.

For over two years and even in moments of solitude, I was hooked on this celebrity trial and obsessed with conflict like much of the world! To me, it symbolized a Shakespearean drama!

Had I known that listening to *The People vs Simpson* would trigger feelings of severe depressions, stress disorder and racial tensions within me that would threaten the foundation of my own spiritual and emotional stability, I would have adhered to a quotation my parents taught me when I was in the first grade: "Never let anyone drag you so low as to make you hate him."

My mind told me that I hated O.J.; but my heart kept telling me to hate the crime, not the person. It was a huge, spiritual order that seemed impossible because I hated the person and the crime. Then, like a frightened child, my humbled heart began searching for the trials' spiritual message. Love is hard work.

Wrestling with writer's block triggered by hurt feelings stemming from domestic abuse, I sat at the computer, waiting, my mind racing back into a childhood world of violent past experiences, both racial and domestic. "Would the Simpson trials be a gauge of race relations or domestic abuse?" I asked myself. In my opinion, they would spark a worldwide discussion about domestic violence and about race relations, bringing them to the forefront. Seeing this as a united people evolving, we will let the healing begin, embracing Nicole and Ron's death as "a monument to human brotherhood."

For therapeutic reasons, and at the beginning of the Simpson case, I had shared with my analyst a terrifying experience similar to this tragedy by writing about it, because to vocally describe it was like reliving the horror of a childhood nightmare. The case was triggering a recurrence of agitated depressions, and for unknown reasons I was in a state of denial regarding the roots of these depressions, knowing that I, too, was once an abused wife.

And now I sat, locked into another phase of writer's block and reading the manuscript I had written while wrestling to work through a previous writer's block. I sat there reading chapters which I had written when I developed a hungry, curious, questing mind that sought answers from my experiences...to open doors that would swing wide to unlimited horizons of knowledge, wisdom and inspiration that would enlarge my understanding of the Simpson Trials.

I began with the chapter that spoke of my therapy sessions and continued reading through the vast storehouse of my experiences.

2

"The human heart is an ever present close friend and guide; it is the cradle of all feelings."

JUST READING FROM THE HEART...

How vividly I recall that once-upon-a-therapy-session in the late fall of 1994 when I was angrily discussing the Simpson trial and the "not-so-justice" system vs the violence of American slavery, my Caucasian analyst of nineteen years, Dr. Kensinger, suggested that I use my therapy and analyze the educational aspects of the case. I told him that I would much rather revisit the book of *Genesis* and gain some insight into man's human nature and the political order.

In a calming voice he further counseled, "Although the Simpson trial exploits, it's educational and therapeutic; so, Alice, try to focus on the wisdom you're learning from it."

He made this statement after I had tearfully told him about

my beloved playmother who was abused by her husband, and that the Simpson trial had awakened my deep fear and pain which stemmed from my experience as a battered wife. Using my therapy, I had written the following excerpt from my own childhood experiences triggered by The Trial of the Century. In this excerpt, which I did not fully share with the analyst because of the age-old adage, *Never tell Whitefolks all your business*, I was flushing out the hurt as part of the mind/body healing process of mounting depressions, pouring from my heart.

"I remember when I was six-years-old, and in the first grade, my beautiful, ebony-complexioned 17-year old playmother was brutally shot and killed by her 35-year old charming, wealthy, half-White angry husband, Jason, and found in a puddle of blood inside the gate of her mother's front yard. Everyone knew Jason and Patty were madly in love with each other; and he was exceptionally kind to her! After blowing his beloved wife's brains out, Jason was terrified of being sent to prison or the chain gang. So, he spent forty days and nights hiding in South Carolina's Cedar Swamp to escape being prosecuted. Being the handsome, wealthy, illegitimate son of the Caucasian sheriff, he did not serve time for the killing, even though he boldly confessed to committing it because, according to him, 'she had no business playing around.'

"About six years later, Jason fell in love and got married again, this time to my older sister's tenth-grade classmate, Margo, who thought Jason was God. Jason and Margo had a fabulous wedding and he treated his 16-year old second wife like royalty. And in less than a year he, raging with anger and jealousy because he again felt that 'she was playing around,' slaughtered Margo with a dull switchblade knife, and dumped her lace, nightgown-clad body into Cedar Swamp's murky water. He skipped town, then returned three years later when it seemed the community's shock had calmed.

"Months later, and looking more handsome and gentlemanly than ever, Jason married the deceased second wife's attractive first cousin, Wanda, who was my eleventh-grade classmate and who worshiped him.

Two months after being married to Wanda, he brutally sliced her throat and dumped her butchered body in Lelia Thicket under the same sycamore tree where we as children often played in our treehouse as 'Rich Whitefolks with long, silky hair'...(the hair was made from cornsilk which we pulled from the ears of corn we striped from cornstalks in Mr. Kribb's cornfield). Jason said he killed Wanda 'because she was playing around.' But he didn't run away this time because he was weary of hiding in the murky swamps and thickets cluttered with rattlesnakes and copperhead snakes slithering about with their venom. So, he was finally sent to prison at his own request and, many years later, died there."

After relating this experience to my analyst without telling him that the three young ladies were all beautiful, dark brown and shapely, I asked, "Wasn't this an urgent cry for help that fell on deaf ears of our society?... our legal system?"

He cleared his throat and paused. Then tugging at his silk, gray necktie, he gently asked, "Well, what do you think?" His tall, medium-built frame moved toward the mahogany desk of the modern furnished Coral Gables office.

Sitting opposite the desk and facing him, I frowned and stared into the sea-blue eyes that I had learned to trust. "Why do you psychiatrists always answer the patient's questions with the patient's questions?" I asked, twisting a button on my white Nolan Miller suit.

He smiled. "I would suggest you answer that one."

Aware that the answers are within myself, I still wanted his professional counseling. "Using my therapy and looking at it now with spiritual understanding, I see a society that still needs help because of footprints of slavery," I said tearfully.

"What do you mean?" he calmly asked, leaning forward in his brown, leather executive chair, his fingers scissored.

"I'm sure the three murders were a serious cry for help by all families involved. And especially Jason's mother. I think she was the sheriff's housemaid. The neighbors said that Jason was a control-freak like his father whose great grandparents were slaveholders.

The doctor shrugged.

Reluctantly, I continued. "I'm sure Jason didn't know he was a control-freak but, that's not important. What's important is that he should've been taught in childhood to treat others as he himself wished to be treated. Good family relationships are always very important because violent children usually come from a violent home environment where this universal golden rule is not lived!"

"Research has found this to be true," he said, nodding.

"But the cry for help, just like many others, is still falling on deaf ears. We need to help stop domestic violence in the home. And by being good examples ourselves, we can nip it at the roots." I was thirsty for the trials spiritual message.

"Then why not use your therapy and write about domestic violence?" he asked.

"You made that suggestion over a decade ago; nobody cares about women being abused," I said quietly, my eyes distant.

"Now that the Simpson case has brought it to the forefront, you can help by being a voice for your deceased playmother and other abused women, including yourself. Don't you consider yourself a good example of a survivor?"

Twisting the lace-trimmed handkerchief in my hand and fighting back tears, I knew he had reference to my ex-husband, Elmo. "It may sound pathetic but it was only recently that I acknowledged being a victim of domestic abuse. Like most women, I've always been in a state of denial because nobody cared about angry men beating hell outta their helpless wives."

"Denial, Alice, is one of the characteristics of battered women?"

I wanted to tell him that even if I tried to write away the pain, I couldn't do it because I now had writer's block. Then, running my fingers through my curly perm, I charged, "Can't do it. I don't want to write about hate. I'd rather write about *Symbols of Love*....a book I started writing a decade ago, remember?"

"Very well."

"'*Symbols of Love*' had to do with my loving parents. My mother taught me the joy of loving the Creator when she was carrying me in her womb. The way she used to sing and shout His praises, I probably was curled up inside her warm body singing and trying to shout with her. Kicking and shouting with joy! That's why I screamed in tears 'Wh-y-y-y-y!' upon arrival."

He smiled. "Then write about your playmother who also was a symbol of love."

The heavy feeling in my heart escalated. "She's definitely a symbol of love, but I don't want to write about her nor her battered life."

"Why?" he asked.

"Because there's far too much violence in this world that stems from feelings of hate toward one another... programmed hate that we're failing to research because it would shake the foundation of adult fragile egos!"

Following the pensive silence, I continued, "We've been repeatedly taught that the meaning of life is to experience love in ourselves and others, and that we came here to recreate with the Creator by extending love."

Then pausing to focus the thoughts that were truly disturbing me, I said, "When my playmother was killed by a husband who actually loved and worshiped her, and everyone knew he loved and worshiped her, I began to question this jealous, conditional love that stinks like the inflated, selfish ego! The ego can be hell! How can a husband beat on a wife whom he loves when he knows that love is expressed through kindness and concern?"

"Perhaps not everyone actually realizes that love's expressed through kindness and concern," he calmly said with elbows resting on the arms of the executive chair, his fingers cupping his chin.

"How else is it expressed? You learn that at home and in Sunday School. You treat others as you wish to be treated! Everyone wants to be treated with kindness and concern. To hell with the expensive material gifts! We wives want the spiritual gifts first! The spiritual gifts are fruits of the spirit: kindness, concern, forgiveness, patience, understanding and what have you! That's the bonding process in any marital relationship."

"Just as you've always said, man is evolving, and it's our mission to help each other evolve. Let's remember that every adversity carries with it the seed of an equivalent benefit."

"Well, I need to find the equivalent benefit that comes from this 'Case of the Century' because, nowadays, every time I hear of a woman being abused, I feel abused!"

"You'll find it; just keep writing. Are you still afraid to speak out against domestic violence?"

When he asked this, I recalled the 17-year-long fear of being stalked by my abusive ex-husband and which therapy had healed. I now wondered was the doctor referring to the incident. I was a bundle of bad nerves!

"I'm not afraid of speaking out against violence of any kind, especially racism," I said dismally, shaking my head in frustration as my negative racial attitude with ingredients of the Simpson trial, American slavery and the Holocaust began to surface. "But writing about such heartbreaking childhood experiences at this time is too confusing and painful."

"Therapy is painful," he counseled, "but it's a process of growing."

Days later and thinking about my analyst's statement that the Simpson Trial, though exploitative, is educational and therapeutic, I was beginning to feel free in helping to flush out the cobwebs of domestic abuse from its well-kept closet of shame, denial and fear. Beyond racism, I was ready to take a more serious look at violence in general to better understand the root of our human behavior. And after experiencing the Simpson case, I'm sure we all want to know why do racism and the notion of white supremacy serve to divide the masses of Black and White people?

Religiously, I continued following the case in spite of the

stress it entailed and the deep feelings of depressions I was encountering. Based on experiences, anyone could see that the colorful, spectacular drama was creating a culture hooked on celebrity trials and obsessed with conflict with the emotions. William Shakespeare was known for this famous school of thought. "Are we back into the Elizabethan period?" I paused and asked the universe.

We all love Shakespeare's genius, and the Simpson trial brought with it all the ingredients of a Shakespearean tragedy.

Perhaps I should have listened to my analyst when he suggested over a decade ago...around 1983... that as a victim of wife abuse, I could write on the subject of domestic violence because it was beginning to be an issue of deep concern.

"After all," he had counseled following my reluctance to tackle the subject, "it was you who wrote in your book, *Mysterious Stranger Aboard*, that your knife-toting ex-husband chased you all over your Atlanta neighborhood attempting to cut off your head with a machete and dump it in a waste basket on Hunter Street. Your whole manuscript portrays emotional scenes of domestic violence, wouldn't you agree? "

Certainly I agreed, although I was not conscious of this while writing. But, I felt insulted by the analyst's truth, and now understood the age-old adage that kept haunting me: "*Never tell Whitefolks all your business*."

But I had to tell him all of my business this time because I had come too far to let The Case of the Century send me back into a miserable state of agitated depression from which I had, through years of psychotherapy, recovered.

How strange that I was able to come this far without revealing the details of being a victim of an abusive marriage and then all of a sudden the buried pain within me exploded when the Simpson case came aboard. Sinking back into depression, I kept identifying with the victim of wife abuse. The doctor sensed this attitude and suggested that I ease the hurt by writing my thoughts and feelings in a journal. I recalled the one I wrote concerning my first marriage and how I cried throughout the writing. In the journal, I referred to my ex-husband as Elmo. The mind/body medicine read thus:

My first husband, Elmo, whom I married in 1952, was a mulatto with silky hair and a World War 11 veteran. To me there was nothing more fascinating than seeing an attractive dark-skinned girl with her half-white colored man with silky hair as sweethearts...like the half-white, silky-haired US Congressman Adam Clayton Powell and his beautiful dark-complexioned concert pianist wife, Hazel Scott. It was common to see a blue-black man with a half-white wife. But to see a blue-black woman with a half-white husband was rare. Colored preachers, concerned about their offsprings, were known to marry mulatto wives with long curly hair instead of dark skinned ones with kinky (super-curly) hair. We get our values from our preachers. They lead, we follow because their guidance comes from a higher source.

Elmo made me feel like an Egyptian queen when we were courting, and he respected my virginity. His kind mulatto mother was happy for us and treated me like a precious jewel. She told me that she had never seen her baby boy...her Elmo... so madly in love with anyone. Naturally, I felt honored. Even Elmo's brothers were overly excited about the engagement because Elmo was their precious baby brother and he was marrying a 'cute little' school teacher.

Two months following the beautiful wedding, doo-doo hit the fan. My Elmo had lied like hell to me about his good character and employment. I was not aware that he was an alcoholic! His loving mother said, "Had you asked me, Alice, I would have told you that he's a very heavy drinker. Some men are still babies, as soon as they put down one bottle they pick up another! But when he met you, he stopped drinking and we all were so glad that you had made him so happy!" She said they all were so happy that Elmo had " found himself a wonderful Christian wife!"

How would I had known to ask about alcohol addiction when I had never seen Elmo drinking, nor did I smell the stuff on him? Was his love for me so powerful that he stopped drinking? I suppose it was, but I was dumbfounded. It undoubtedly was the grace of God speaking to both of us. Then what happened? Not knowing at that time that life is a series of problem solving situations, I did not get the spiritual message nor did I understand how to deal with our financial situation when his drinking began consuming our income, and my efforts to save the marriage seemed fruitless.

Inasmuch as the purpose of money is to finance life, and he had been all this time living off his mother's income and wasting his, he had a difficult time shouldering his part of the responsibilities. In his struggle to get a better paying job, he applied to the post office but was repeatedly turned down. Yes, he was turned down job after job. He had no creditability and only a high school education (he told me that he dropped out of college in his senior year). He was very depressed. Added to this insult to Elmo's male ego, he couldn't make payments to the store for my engagement ring and the store garnisheed my teaching check. Because of this, I was fired from the Paulding County school system. And now I, too, was jobless and deeply depressed. Luckily, I was employed at another school in Fulton County but as a school secretary. Being a neophyte, I encountered difficulties and the typing errors were atrocious. When Elmo realized how frustrated I was, he went to the principal's house, half drunk, and wanted to punch him out for making me so frustrated on the new job. The principal's beautiful, caring mother heard all the commotion and attempted to call the police that this drunk fool was attacking her son. Out of respect for me, the principal begged her not to call the cops, and that he would dismiss me. And now I was again jobless because of Elmo. Through a close friend, Mr. Cochran, the kind principal found a secretarial position for me at the Young Men's Christian Association off Auburn Avenue and near Ebenezer Baptist Church where Dr. Martin Luther King's father pastored. Mr. Warren Cochran, who was the executive director of the YMCA and who was aware of my financial problems, was instrumental in helping Elmo and me get help through YMCA board member Attorney Walden. "Caring adults helping young married couples," Elmo and I said in prayerful gratitude.

Number two: When we were courting, Elmo swore he was co-owner of Richard's Dry Cleaners, and even the owner, overjoyed about the engagement, said that he was. Elmo was a hard working employee there who worked the dry cleaner's press machines and earned $30 a week. When I learned this, I had no problem with it because we could work hard, save our money and open our own dry cleaning business inasmuch as he was very good at the trade. But, we couldn't save any money because he would spend it all on whiskey. In addition, he kept causing me to lose my jobs when all my life I've had a job and had never been fired from one until he came aboard. I was brought up working in Whitefolks cotton, tobacco and corn fields. I worked my way through college and often made honor roll in the process. Perhaps he and I had different perceptions about responsible employment to help finance one's life.

Elmo did work hard at helping to save our marriage in spite of the power of whiskey. He was drawn to God and joined the huge Baptist church on West Hunter where I was a Sunday School teacher, an ardent member of the Young Adult Choir, and a member of the Pastor's Aid Society. It was "the love of God inside of my sweet hard working wife," he told friends, "that led me to join the church." It made me feel humble to be a part of his salvation.

On the Sunday when he was scheduled to be baptized at the evening services (and as I'm writing this, tears are flooding my eyes), instead of being with him following the morning church services, I was at the Pastor's Aid Society meeting all that afternoon discussing fund-raising projects. When I left the meeting and rushed home to go with my Elmo to the evening services at which he was to be submerged in a pool of water, he had already caught the city bus and gone back to church. I'll never forget the sadness and humbleness in his eyes when I arrived at church and apologized to him for being late. He looked at me sadly and said: "I expected you to be with me because this was so special to me." I stood there in tears; my heart heavy with pain as I apologized to God and him for my insensitiveness. And as I write this, all I can hear is the song that he, so sadly, would always sing ... "I Surrender All" .. because it was sung while he was being submerged in water, accepting Christ as his Savior.

Why didn't I continue to stand by him after we had come this far and he was trying so hard to fight an alcohol addiction? I tried to stand by him but I needed more help from the Creator. It seemed the alcohol was making him far happier than 'De Lord.' No one told me about Alcoholics Anonymous, not even the minister who admitted being an alcoholic prior to becoming a preacher. Anyway, when my Elmo couldn't fight off the addiction, and I seemed powerless to help him, he became discouraged. He gave up trying and returned again to spending all the money to support his drinking habit. Our financial security was ruined. We worked harder and prayed as frustrations mounted. He became angry and his anger made him abusive. Sometimes in his drunkened anger, he would chase me all over the neighborhood with a switchblade knife and the neighbors would hide me in their clothes closets. His anger sparked jealousy, and he accused me of having an affair with a college professor at the university where I was now a graduate student and a faculty secretary after losing my YMCA secretarial position. In his raging anger and throughout the three-year marriage, he continued to drink heavily and often threatened my life. I left him three times and returned because he wanted and needed me and I felt sympathy for his addiction...a sickness, and his state of financial insecurity. I realized it was difficult for a Black man to get a decent job in a White society until he could begin his own business. Often times businesses are passed down from one generation to another and this unifies the family. His family worked hard, but like my family, there was no family business. Being financially broke can add more hell to an already troubled marriage; and we became more and more insecure. We were so broke, we "couldn't even pay attention" to the universe which teaches that difficulties build strength. We were desperately depressed and poor but we were hanging-on while we tried to find work for him. And now, I had a job at the university as secretary to the dean in the School of Education.

One day, feeling disgusted, hopeless and depressed he exploded in a raging fit of anger, then shoved in my face a Jet magazine's gruesome picture of a Black girl's bloody, severed head lying on top of a garbage can on a busy Chicago street. He bitterly shouted, "Take a good look at this butchered head, you bitch, 'cause your's gonna look just like it when I finish slaughtering you and dumping your head in that garbage can on Hunter Street!" Trembling with fear, I prayed in silence, frightened for both of us that we were getting nowhere fast except to our graves.

And then it almost happened. Following this vicious warning, I came face to face with death. It happened like this: One Sunday when I spent the day at the university typing a graduate student master's thesis to supplement our income, Elmo became enraged, snatched his machete from the closet shelf and was ready for my head. When I came home, I walked right into his anger and, as the Creator would have it, his mother called via telephone. While he was talking with her, I ran from the house as fast as I could to my neighbor's apartment down the street. She was ironing in her living room. Quickly, she hid me in her clothes closet, hurriedly called the police, then proceeded with her ironing. Nervously, I warned her that my husband was exploding with so much anger that he would kill her for being in the way while he was coming for my head. She boldly said "Let him bring his ass in here and I'll shove this hot iron right into his s—color face!"

While I was at the neighbor's house, and Elmo was still combing the neighborhood looking for me, I hurriedly called his mother who said she was coming right away to protect me; and begged me not to put those cruel White policemen on her baby because they would kill him and think nothing about it.

I didn't want anyone killing Elmo because I understood and saw his anger. But I also saw my sawed-off head on top of that garbage can on Hunter Street. And with my attorney's advice I got the hell out of that house, flew out of Georgia and back to my Mother's house in South Carolina, leaving everything behind. So afraid that he would find me, I lived in a world of fear for my family and for me.

The Atlanta sheriff served a warrant on Elmo while I was in South Carolina trembling with fear. After months of Elmo's serious threats and stalking, I got a divorce and the stalking and threats continued. He swore he was gonna get me regardless of where I lived. While I was living in the university dormitory the following year, Elmo rented a room in an apartment house across the street from the dorm, directly in front of the dorm's main exit. The landlady noticed he was acting peculiar as though he were stalking someone coming out of the dormitory. She called the university president who investigated the situation, then he called the dormitory matron. The matron broke the news to me. I was shocked and frightened beyond words that Elmo lived across the street and expected the university to demand that I move elsewhere (i.e. that you take your domestic violence elsewhere). But instead, the president had the landlady get rid of Elmo because his being there was endangering the lives of hundreds of other students who also lived in that dormitory.

I fell to my knees, thanking the Creator for such caring and concerned individuals.

Once-upon-another-time when I was enroute back to the dorm after choir practice, Elmo ran up behind me with a knife and threaten to cut my throat and throw my body over the six-foot high wall of shrubbery onto the university's neatly manicured grounds. Although I was nervous, I acceded to the advice of Attorney *Walden who counseled: "Whenever Elmo's threatening you, say nothing and don't act as though you're afraid of him."*

The legal counseling worked.

It was in 1975 while in therapy when I told Dr. Kensinger that I feared my ex-husband was still stalking me. Through counseling, the doctor was able to rid me of this paranoia. I was so glad to be free of this fear. And now here comes "The Trial of the Century," and I was beginning to relive the experience of being an abused wife all over again because I was too afraid to "tell Whitefolks all my business." I was ready to gladly sweep all of these buried fears out of my system. My tears are for all abused women.

I felt equally insulted by our African American attorney friend, Neil, who happens to be an activist, when he objected to my being counseled by a Caucasian analyst and had harshly asked, "What the hell can a White man tell a Black woman about her depressions?"

Angered by this insult, I fired back, "My analyst said that he doesn't see color, he sees an individual who needs help."

To this, Neil replied, "Really? I bet he's filthy rich, drives a white Rolls- Royce with white on white in white, and lives in his mansion in the richest section of Coconut Grove where the signs read: 'no niggers allowed.'"

My husband, John, had chuckled and it infuriated me to the extent that I fired back: "For your information, Neil, the 'White' analyst is telling me the joy of loving, respecting and appreciating my husband and people of all faiths, races and nationalities! And listen, Neil, just as I told you earlier, I don't give a damn about your brand of racism!"

He snapped back, "And I don't give a damn about your brand of chicken soup!"

I suppose my scholarly husband, John, being a Morehouse College graduate, asked himself the same question. He had told Neil that our analyst was "filthy-rich and drives a white Rolls-Royce and lives in the rich section of Miami's Coconut Grove!" Perhaps that's why my husband felt tip-top and justified in being "a therapy dropout" when it was he and his multiple sclerosis...which we called the mysterious stranger (MS)... that needed the therapy. I was an innocent caregiving victim. But it was the universe's blessing that I was a part of the triangle...John, MS and me (more about this later). But then, John and I had two Jaguars (cars not animals) and living in a well-to-do lily-white neighborhood (now populated with well-to-do South Americans), which proved that we, like every hard-working American, love and enjoy a taste of the good life.

My thoughts again returned to the question our militant colleague had asked and that had angered me to the point of calling his question "a brand of racism." He had retaliated by accusing me of "drowning in chicken soup" when I spoke in defense of the White analyst.

Although defensive of the analyst whom I had learned to trust and who, to me, represented the basic kindness of the White race as well as the basic kindness of all races in general, I partially agreed with the activist. On the other hand, after giving this serious thought, I could not help but recall our African American elementary school principal's famous quote regarding the theory of understanding one another: *If you don't know from where I'm coming, how do you know where I'm going?*

I paused to get a cup of decaffeinated coffee, then continued my reading.

"When we consider the subject of crime and human nature, could we all have come from the roots of *Genesis?*" I now asked the universe. "Does crime result from individual choice?" If so, then why did you let the Roman soldiers crucify Jesus when he taught nothing but love?"

Even so, I was grateful that the analyst did not mention how my gentlemanly second husband, John, in 1979, angered, confused and abusive because of his debilitating illness, multiple sclerosis...sometimes called MS...had attempted to blow my brains out. Why? Because he feared that I was overspending our dwindling savings. The government had repeatedly denied him compensation in spite of all the documentation sent by his doctors to the Board of Veterans Appeals. He was heartbroken. The MS had flared up while he was in the Korean War and stationed in cold/hot Korea. John had chronic fears that because of his failing health, we were financially, mentally and emotionally headed for bankruptcy, or to resort to welfare. It was our good friend, a Caucasian Catholic nun, who had intervened with her prayers that saved our hides from this tragedy. Thanks to the universe for our good friend's visit at that time; she saved our lives...probably her's, too.

In addition, our visiting nun, through actions of love, was instrumental in our writing, almost two decades later, a sequel to

Mysterious Stranger Aboard, a euphemism for MS Aboard. The title of the sequel... *Love Paints Beauty In The Soul*, was the result of our being awakened to the basic goodness in all humanity.

Our 40-year battle with multiple sclerosis had brought us to the stage of enlightenment in which we saw God in man.

Several paths led to this enlightenment. One of them is as follows: After the near tragedy my husband and I had with the gun, we told our analyst about what had happened and what triggered the fighting rage. Especially his painful disappointment that VA had denied him compensation for his total disability and he feared for our financial future. It was our analyst who immediately counseled that my husband and I get rid of the gun. It was also our analyst who, in 1975, encouraged us to write our thoughts and feelings as a form of therapy to cope with frustrations stemming from John's illness...a crippling disease of the central nervous system that robs motor skills, and for which there is yet no cure.

We followed his wise counseling and became obsessed with writing our thoughts and feelings. Writing became our survival tool and a powerful, learning instrument that enabled us to find our innerselves. Doing this promoted our spiritual growth. For my husband and me, writing became an excellent form of meditation that bonded our marriage with love and mutual respect for each other.

Through writing, I uncovered layers and layers of physical and mental domestic abuse and racial violence buried in my world of experiences. The awakening astounded me inasmuch as I thought it was a way of life combined with another form of slavery...American style... woven into the fiber of our society.

So excited at that time about the awakening of our newfound creative writing skills, I began retyping a novel entitled *Kennetta* which I started writing while we were residing in Ohio. This was around 1965, before John's MS was diagnosed. I had stopped writing the novel because John, in a fit of rage, had shoved the typewriter off the dining room table and screamed, "I don't have a g..d... wife anymore! To hell with your writing!"

John and I now thank the universe that, in 1971, his MS was diagnosed by one of its messengers of love, Dr. Edmund Casey. The diagnosis helped us to understand the cause of John's sometimes violent behavior. We also now thank the universe for its mysterious guidance in moving us from Cincinnati to Miami in 1974 where we were mysteriously helped by its many messengers of love that came in all faiths, races, and nationalities. Messengers who helped us cope with MS, further bonding our love and mutual respect for each other, rescuing us from domestic violence.

And now, back to the discussion of "Kennetta" which I began rewriting in 1976 after discovering via of analysis that writing is a form of therapy. In this emotional novel, I was flushing out age-old cobwebs of wife abuse by telling the true story of a friend of mine but by telling it with a slant. The following synopsis of the story held my attention and kept my mind focused.

The story unfolds in 1940 when the beautiful dark-complexioned pregnant mother, Anabelle, is severely kicked in the stomach by her jobless, angry Creole husband, Kenneth. She rolls beneath the bed to protect her unborn baby. Following the abuse, she is brought to the doctor's office by her apologetic husband who drops her off and speeds away for fear of being reported and jailed. The White male physician, Dr. Kelley, for whom Anabelle serves as housemaid and to whom she dare not tell of the abuse, assumes that she had fallen down the stairs as one of the Caucasian female nurses, herself an abused wife, has reported. With careful supervision, the medical staff helps Anabelle through premature labor. The infant survives, pushing its head through the bloody door as though the muses were hurrying it into a suffering world to help "Stop the violence!" as it had promised before leaving home. "Whi-i-i-i-i?" the infant screamingly asked as the force of nature shoves its tiny body from Anabelle's womb. Undoubtedly, upon returning to earth as requested, it had forgotten its mission. Although Dr. Kelly is astounded that the screaming and kicking infant is alive, he is also disappointed that it is a girl instead of the little boy which he had months ago predicted and they were all expecting. Feeling the need for a sense of humor, he shrieks, "Good heavens, Anabelle, he's a she! Your husband's gonna be mad as hell 'cause he wanted a little Kenneth like himself, not another girl!" Anabelle, too, is disappointed but too weak to respond. Feeling alarmed that women have to suffer the pain of childbearing and those (biblically unclean) monthly periods, Dr. Kelley clears his throat then quotes a Jewish morning prayer, "'Blessed be God that He did not make me a woman.'" Taken aback by the prayer that, to her, made men feel superior to women, Anabelle tearfully retaliates "Blessed be the Lord, who created my baby according to His will." Two days later, Anabelle dies with the sickly infant held closely in her arms. The baby is adopted by the kind doctor and his 25-year old attractive attorney wife, Dee Dee, who is an advocate of Women's rights and a follower of Simone DeBeauvoir school of thought. They name the infant "Kennetta" and shower her with love because of their love for Anabelle whose own parents and grandparents were Dee Dee's parents and grandparents' maids since the days of American slavery. While being raised and educated with the Kelleys two children, Doris and Joey, Kennetta becomes aware of frustrating racial barriers but Dee Dee encourages her to rise and feel good about herself in spite of the barriers. With this powerful encouragement, Kennetta, like Joey and Doris, graduates from Harvard Law School in which she earns a degree in Criminal Law. Kennetta happily marries a wealthy, real estate businessman, Walt Debash, who worships her and resembles her Creole father. Unlike Kennetta, Walt is an ambitious social climber. They have three lovely children...two boys and a girl. For ten years, theirs is a model family of love, laughter and a host of friends. Then, Walt becomes fearful that Kennetta and her law firm partner, Joey, are fiery lovers and that the unborn baby Kennetta is now carrying is not his. Enraged with jealousy, Walt accuses his pregnant wife of having an affair with Joey, the childhood playmate with whom she and Doris once-upon-a-time enjoyed playing "Doctor."

The marriage explodes into a battlefield, and Kennetta becomes a battered wife. She understands her Walt's anger because she understands the flight of a successful, ambitious Black man in White society during this Civil Rights period. Aware that Walt is using his anger with her as a scapegoat for his anger with White society, she fights to save the marriage. Years later, the marriage worsens when he loses the position of county commissioner to a male Hispanic. In her struggle to hold the marriage for the sake of the children, Kennetta enters the battered women's shelter three times. She divorces and remarries Walt three times. Mentally and emotionally bankrupted, and still helplessly in love with Walt, she storms out of the marriage and seeks help from the National Coalition Against Domestic Violence (NCADV) of which Dee Dee is a legal advisor. As a single mother with three children in college and one in senior high, she emerges strong, brave and together, determined to join the fight against domestic violence in behalf of all battered women. Will she be successful in doing this or will she continue a victim due to human nature and the political order? Stay tuned.

Unfortunately, I laid *Kennetta* aside in 1982 to continue work on *Mysterious Stranger Aboard* because we were living with the abusive mysterious stranger...MS... and needed to understand how to successfully shift gears and continue our bonding and spiritual growth. For our own health, we first needed to write about what was actually going on in our everyday marriage triangle...John, MS and me. The process of writing it was a mind/body medicine and a mysterious blessing for us that enriched our souls and saved us from domestic abuse in the process.

We worked on *Mysterious Stranger Aboard* and completed it in 1993, following Hurricane Andrew's vicious onslaught that destroyed our South Dade community and many of our lives...emotionally, economically and physically.

John and I stated in *Mysterious Stranger Aboard*: "*Miraculously, only 38 deaths related to the hurricane were reported in South Florida* *where over 45 million people reside. However, in terms of property destruction, Hurricane Andrew was the worse disaster ever to befall the United States. Its grim toll totaled $20 billion in damages...in more human terms, over 63,000 homes were destroyed (most of them in South Dade) and over 100,000 were damaged. Over 250,000 people were left homeless; John and I were among them. The Veterans Administration Medical Center moved quickly to place my totally disabled husband in its nursing home while I wrestled with the excessive stress of rebuilding our home."*

Again, and via Hurricane Andrew, the universe spoke through its mysterious language by showing us love in action as we recovered with the help of its messengers of love who came from all faiths, races, and nationalities to help put the lives of all us suffering South Floridians back together and continue our spiritual journey of evolving as a people united. This outpouring of universal love was also one of the experiences that influenced us in writing the sequel to our book and giving it the title *Love Paints Beauty in the Soul*.

Suddenly, and as the universe would have it because the present life is one of conflict with the emotions, another battle with the human spirit erupted as a strange new mystery came ashore...The Trial of the Century.

In June of 1994 when *The People vs Simpson* case took center stage in American society and became an obsession and a learning institution within itself, I questioned the obsession and its meaning. Undoubtedly, we need to examine our moral and spiritual values, I thought to myself, adhering to the theory: "Trust life and it will teach you." We women were grateful that the case was placing domestic violence, at last, on the front burner.

The case brought with it unusual stress seasoned with bouts of depression that continued to mount in proportion with its mysteriousness, crimes of society, and human nature. It was obvious that we Americans were being divided between racial lines and this ignited confusion, misunderstanding, anger, hate, jealousy, deceit, greed, and all the instruments of fear that can destroy faith in each other and in humanity, and a loss of respect and appreciation for our multiculturalness. It seemed we were missing the target.

"Man is a social animal and is meant for social living," my analyst had counseled many therapy-sessions ago. "He has a nature that reflects to a degree heritable traits and possesses a perception of good and evil (i.e. love and hate)." I realized that it is the perception of what's good and evil that both requires and makes possible our ability to live together as an immediate family, as a community, and as a united people. Aren't we yet evolving?

"Write out your feelings," my analyst had counseled in the early stages of the trial when I seemed more focused on the case, the violence and the racial hatred that seemed to be surfacing than on my own search for innerself...the sources of inner happiness and psychic wholeness. "You must keep writing to let those feelings surface. It's for your own good health," he suggested.

Confused, I had replied with a tinge of anger, "For health reasons I did write my deepest feelings, doctor! And for your information I shared them with fellow students in our UM creative writing course that meets at Border's Bookstore in Kendall!"

Silence swelled, then I continued, adding that the 800-word prose-in-poetry was entitled O. J. University. "But, doctor, I was shocked to learn that I am the only one in the class who strongly thinks O.J. , though guilty of the battering, is innocent of the murders! And that he was framed. The class commented that my 'prose-in-poetry' was creatively written and highlighted insightful moral and spiritual values about the case. Then slowly, they all gave me a hard, cold stare. One of them stated unflinchingly, 'Alice Johnson, O.J. is as guilty as sin of domestic abuse and of those double murders!' And the rest of my classmates totally agreed with her! I felt angry and responded defensively, 'But the trial has just started! In our American democracy, anyone is considered innocent until proven guilty!' Their hard stare turned to ice cubes, and I got the feeling that they wanted the system to win and punish, not give justice. 'Case closed', I said dejectedly and they seconded the motion. For the first time I *actually* realized that I was the only Black in the predominately White class. And all this time, I was thinking we were writers, not colors. But, I refused to feel like the little black sheep who had lost its way in understanding human nature and the political order. Especially when one of my male classmates started reciting the nursery rhyme: 'Humpty Dumpty sat on the Wall...Humpty Dumpty had a great fall.. All the king's horses and all the king's men couldn't put Humpty together again.'"

My analyst had smiled, then quickly changed the subject and asked how was my hospitalized husband.

I blurted out, "My husband hopes that O. J's innocent of the double murders, too! He feels deeply depressed that his favorite sports celebrity is guilty of wife abuse just as many well-meaning husbands sometimes are when they momentarily explode in uncontrolled anger. But he feels that O.J. has far too much to lose by resorting to murdering two innocent people. My husband watches the case religiously from his VA hospital bed and his wheelchair."

With furrowed brow, the analyst then asked, "Don't you feel that due to his illness, the case is too stressful for him to watch?"

Shrugging, I staunchly said, "You suggested that I not censor his TV programs, remember?"

He replied, kneading his forehead, "But, I was under the impression that you would use your therapy in making the choices."

Bepuzzled, I replied, "But, doctor, I was using my therapy! You said the TVs in the courtroom could make the trial educational and therapeutic!"

Silence again swelled and I felt a tinge of anger.

"Whitefolks!" I scoffed silently, my ego inflating, then stormed from the office with a throbbing headache because I sensed...in my brand of racism... that he, too, like his lily-White counterparts and my lily-White best friends, and my lily-White classmates as well as our lily-White priest and parishioners, believed O.J. to be "guilty as sin of the domestic abuse and the double murders" even though he had no body bruises on him nor was he soaked in spilled blood!"

I wanted to tell my analyst that I had even sent a copy of my "Prose-in-Poetry" to TV-Channel 7 because I was obsessed with their sensational educational reporting of the case, and that my good friend, Sally, had said they probably flushed it down the toilet because I believed the famous hero innocent.

For good reasons, I was beginning to feel uncomfortably divided even among the handful of Blacks who insisted on prejudging the case. Aware that it is unfair to try controlling others thoughts and feelings, I did feel that the attitude of prejudging was wrong, and thought it unfair to kick a man who is already down and fighting for his life.

There were so many questions that needed answering. Why weren't there bruises or marks on O.J. Simpson's body? Why did the most DNA come from the bloodstains that showed up for the first time weeks after the murders? If the murders began at 10:35 pm, as the evidence showed beyond any doubt, when and how could O.J. could have accomplished them?

I though about Jesus' crucifixion and wondered how much of it was political. I thought about the death of John Kennedy, Martin Luther King, Gandhi. I thought about the Tuskegee experiment...a study in official turpitude that saw the U.S. government perpetrating medical malpractice on African Americans from 1932 to 1972 in the name of research. I thought about the April 1995 Oklahoma City bombing in which 168 victims died, the 1994 seige of the Branch Davidians at Waco, Texas where children were killed, and all the strange happenings here on planet earth. I was beginning to feel more frightened.

I recalled Sally telling me not to be frightened for O.J. because he came from strong stock. She said that during the Civil Rights Movement when her daughter taught language arts and social studies at Galileo High in San Francisco, O.J. was one of her favorite, energetic students. Although he was rebellious and often suspended from school, sometimes ending up in Juvenile Hall, he always respected, Eunice, his religious mother who worked hard to keep her tall, lanky, restless son out of trouble. Eunice, she said, was often referred to as "the praying nun" by church members and co-workers at San Francisco General Hospital psychiatric ward because of the spiritual energy she exerted in working with patients and family. Sally stated that it was Eunice's unshakable faith that molded O. J. into a mystical hero. Even so, I still was frightened and felt it unfair to prejudge O.J. who was now down and fighting for his life.

More painfully, I was unaware that Sally, herself an abused wife, was also fighting desperately for her own life before she died. And now weeping, I recalled one of our last conversations about the trial.

Sally warned that had I been glued to *The Oprah Winfrey Show*, as usual, that teaches self-esteem instead of switching to *The Simpson Trial* that was driving everybody nuts, I wouldn't now be fighting for my sanity. I should have listened to her warning.

CHAPTER TWO

The love of our neighbor is the essential action of human existence.
-Ladisllaus Boros, S.J.
September, 1995

"Frightened? Simpson's not already down; so stop acting like a fool, girlfriend!" a petite and feisty Sally said to me once-upon-a-healthwalk in mid-September 1995. We were discussing the Trial of the Century during one of our 7 am five-mile brisk strolls in Miami's Coral Reef Park. Florida warblers chirped among landscaped evergreens as we kept in step.

Sally, who to me resembled shapely singer-actress Patty LaBelle in physique and personality, ran her fingers through permed shoulder-length hair and continued talking. "O.J.'s cool, calm and together but somebody oughta kick his behind for beating on his pretty little wife who bore for him those two darling children."

I agreed, feeling that I needed my behind kicked, too, for being obsessed with the case. Then, grabbing a handful of bread crumbs from the bag I was carrying, I paused to feed the grey duck and ducklings that were wobbling toward us as Sally continued talking into my thirst for spiritual understanding.

"And, girlfriend, they said Simpson's a metaphor of the great divide in the whole United States, and the different reality, experiences, viewpoints and worlds in which we Blackfolks and Whitefolks live." She was bubbling with life!

"Metaphor?" I asked as we continued walking. "Maybe he's

from another planet."

"Could be. And, girlfriend, I question these Black church members giving O.J. money when the Good Lord can't even collect from these stingy folks His own little ten-percent due Him."

I laughed. "Maybe the Juice is a messenger, Sally."

Sally yelped. "You'd better get outta my face with that crap! Marie Mohammed told me you're missing your mammogram appointments to watch that case on TV when you know that breast cancer runs in your family."

"Get off my case, Sally," I teased.

"You get off his case, girlfriend," she shrieked in her rebuttal. "Cause he's not Blackfolks nohow and you can see that for yourself!"

"Stay off my case, Sally. We're dealing with a trial that offers courses in multicultural education."

But she continued, "And another thing, girlfriend, speaking of multicultural education, you need to turn off that 'TV trial' and start writing those pre-and post-production teaching packets for your docudramas that'll be coming up soon that emphasize multicultural education! We teachers are gonna whip your butt if you don't get them to us since we've made reservations to bring thousands of our students to Dade County Auditorium to see your plays." (They brought over 4,000 that December of 1995).

"I'm writing the docudrama 'Holiday Customs in The International City' for a precelebration of Miami Centennial '96, Sally."

"That's great! We saw the announcement on the schools' E-mail! But we should have those teaching packets in our hands. You oughta be ashamed that you don't have 'em ready for us yet 'cause you're obsessed with that TV circus! What bothers me is that you, of all people, have the audacity to act a fool 'cause I'm not obsessed with the case, too! That's not at all like you! You've always had those teaching packets in our hands by this time!"

When I groaned and expressed my apology, she continued, "I'm gonna tell you like I keep telling my family, you'd better get on with your own life and stop looking at somebody else's 'real life TV soap opera.' My ex-husband, Isaac, was abusive to me, too! Knocking me around trying to control my life! And on top of that, the fool was as poor as Satan 'cause that ring he gave me came outta a Cracker Jack box!"

"Is that why you left him...'cause he was poor and abusive?"

She gaped. "Left him? He left me! Girlfriend, you oughta know for yourself that women who leave their battering husbands are at risk of being killed by the fool more than those who stay!"

"Then, how did you divorce Isaac and get your Frederick you now have?" Even Federick was a wife batterer.

She looked at me and laughed. "The Lord's will, honey. Even though I was married to Isaac, I asked the Lord to send me a good Christian man who loved me!" She stabbed her index finger in her chest. "I wanted somebody who really loved me, not his damn ego! And, girlfriend, the Lord moves in a mysterious way. You know the sign that said 'Love thy neighbor but don't get caught?' Well, my ex-husband did it and got caught by the neighbor's husband who was meaner than him. My ex hightailed it back to Valdosta like a skinned cat when that man blew his wife's brains out with a shotgun and came looking for his behind! Isaac met an older White woman and divorced me so he could marry her 'cause she had money to help him open his law office."

"Sounds like a soap opera."

"Not really 'cause the fool still loves me and it makes Frederick jealous as hell...mad enough to kill us both."

I flinched, recalling my own abusive ex-husband who, because of anger, shot an innocent, unarmed man in the foot. When he told me about it, I felt I hated him. I felt grateful that O.J. was bringing violence and racism to the forefront.

Sally began singing the blues: "*Don't want no man always hitting on me...the last man that hit me's been dead since thirty-three.* It seems the media has already found the innocent man guilty! I've stopped listening to a lot of that stuff the media is reporting 'cause it can drive you nutty and make you dislike and distrust a lot of nice people and the justice system if you haven't an opened mind."

"I try to read though the propaganda and be objective as much as possible."

"That's great, but you can't be going around here with your mind locked in believing that somebody framed O.J. as most of our Black people believe. Most serious minded people, I'm sure, have a reasonable doubt."

I agreed. She told me that the case was trying to affect their relationships among multi-ethnic faculty members at work, but that they had the wisdom to keep their thoughts and feelings to themselves. " Otherwise, there could be a long lasting, silent, racial war raging inside our minds, and I value other people and their friendships..including my students... far too much to let that happen!" she confessed.

Again, I understood and agreed; and could clearly see why I needed to let my mind write what it was thinking rather than share my thoughts with anyone. Personally, I needed to get a better understanding of what the universe was teaching via the Simpson trial, and use it to promote my own spiritual growth. When I told Sally this and how I'm always fascinated by the human experience, and that the case is an institution, she laughed and said, "Girlfriend, you're darn right it's an institution! But from your world, Alice Johnson, you and all these other folks who're obsessed with that case and forgetting about your own are turning it into a mental institution!"

We both laughed, then jumped from the path of two young skaters on roller blades.

Sally ran her fingers through her hair and continued. "I wanted to take a dip in your swimming pool yesterday while you were watching that case on TV , but the water was green. I said, 'Good Lord, even my girlfriend's pool's turned green with envy! 'cause she's too engrossed with TV to at least put a little chlorine in it."

We both laughed, and Sally continued talking, telling me that I shouldn't be worrying myself to death about soul brothers Christopher Darden, the state prosecutor for the trial and Johnnie Cochran, Simpson's defense lawyer, because she felt sure that they would follow their higher consciousness in presenting the case. She suggested that I have faith in the jury system of our democracy.

But I felt uncomfortable with Sally's earlier feelings that although we African-Americans would like to believe that O.J. is innocent of the double murders (but not of the abuse), " O.J. might be lying to us and we are so much in love with the outstanding former brown-skinned handsome football hero to awaken to this. Our support for Simpson might me a big mistake."

Reflecting on the hero, I said, "You must agree, Sally, that the football great was once among the country's favorite sons! The guy was honored for his on-field pro-football analysis, loved for running through airports in commercials, and worshiped for appearing all over the world in movies full of laughs and jokes."

Sally nodded her head in agreement.

"I'm hurt because he was an abusive husband."

"Most of us are, Alice. But who else but a popular celebrity like O.J. could bring domestic violence to the worldwide forefront! Let's face it, girlfriend, prior to this time, no one gave a damn about women being brutally beaten up by their husbands. We need to thank him at least for that much, even if we do have our doubts that he committed those murders and walked away with no bruises and not drenched with blood, and in that limited time slot. But, we'll leave that up to the jury."

"And if the jury has a reasonable doubt like many of us Blacks have so far, that he did it, then it's between Simpson and his Creator."

"Correct! Some people also said O.J.'s mistake was the flair with which he lived with his beautiful wife there in Southern California where the beating of the Black motorist Rodney King took place. With Simpson's naturally handsome self, his fabulous wealth and his popularity, he probably made some racists policemen with lesser means feel he was flaunting his rise in spite of racism and started seeing him as a color."

"Maybe the universe was molding both him and the racist cop for this mission."

Sally groaned. "Child, please!"

"You're not following Biblical history." I paused, then scratched into my perm and continued, "Although I strongly believe that race permeates today's society, we've gotta rise higher and look deeper for the universal, spiritual message. It's such a blessing to be able to rise to your highest potential without other people blocking your path."

"Without the struggle most of us Blacks face, O. J. Simpson was flying higher than an eagle."

"That's why his life as a hero is such a mystery...to think that one could rise so high right here in America regardless of race, color or creed! That's the American dream." Then pausing, I quoted a verse from my O.J. University mind/body medicine:

"He's rich and famous, handsome, gifted; he has charisma, too! .. He is a symbol of 'America's Apple Pie' come true! Shakespeare is famous for great plays of fallen men of fame. Simpson's symbolic of these plays, 'O.J.'s' a famous name! His life's a learning institution, universally. Sometimes his trial seems our trial. Life is a mystery!"

Apprehensive about my lyrics because one of my classmates said they seemed akin to gangsta rap because our hero was found to be a wife abuser, I told Sally that my perceptions were drowning in a world of confusion and frustrations.

"You go, girlfriend," Sally said, throwing her hair from her face. "That's why TV-Channel 7 probably flushed that prose-in-poetry down the toilet."

We both laughed and I said, "That's because racism permeates our society regardless of how much we try to deny it. We need to acknowledge it, kill the evil sin and move forward toward healing our suffering humanity."

"Your point's well taken. And, just like you once said, maybe the universe is trying to tell us all something by human example. O.J. was spared all the suffering and humiliation, all the adversities women and minorities undergo to move ahead in this White male dominated society."

"That's why my husband and I continue to write and produce docudramas on positive role models who, in spite of adversity, rise to their highest potentials to help humanity," I said into the sound of automobiles zooming east and west on Coral Reef Drive. "But, ever since *Genesis*, people have been blocking others paths. And even in the New Testament, they blocked Jesus's path. I need to thoroughly study the book of *Genesis*. This case has me reading the Bible in search of our biblical roots like mad. I've never before searched the Bible with so much seriousness!"

Sally nodded her head, "I've a feeling this case has a lot of folks heads buried in the Bible trying to understand what the Creator's been telling us all along. Violence stems from hate. When you find yourself feeling hate, you know something's wrong inside your heart and you need to clean it up."

"But, Sally, it's been said that we humans are driven by anxiety toward the ideas that deal with the mystery of our ills; and that we've gained the mastery of the material world without knowing ourselves. Why are we a violent people?"

"When we get through with this mess O.J. got us all into, we're gonna be knowing a lot about ourselves, our God and each other."

"I need to revisit Socrates who believed that goodness in a man is based on wisdom, and wickedness is based on ignorance. He said that no wise man would deliberately choose what was bad for him in the long run, but most men, through complete ignorance, may choose an evil that appears to be good at the time."

"You go, girlfriend! But one has to know the principals of right conduct; and Jesus Christ taught us that by example."

"And then he was falsely accused and crucified. Socrates was falsely accused and condemned to death . John the Baptist 's head was cut off because some foolish mother requested it and the sex-crazed king honored the request in lieu of her daughter's who was the king's mistress. Both Gandhi and Martin Luther King were assassinated for speaking up for human rights. Frustrating, isn't it?"

"Not necessarily. They lived noble lives and we follow in their footsteps."

"You're right. Since I too must die, let it be for a noble cause. Women often die for noble causes but their names never go down in the pages of history. That's why I need to study the entire Bible because more and more I find that it speaks to our own life."

"Good! As long as you allow yourself to see beyond organized religions and racial lines."

"A Southern Baptist minister said that *Genesis* requires a verdict, and that's why it's so compelling. He said folks can't read the chapters in *Genesis* and be indifferent to them and..."

Sally interrupted, quickly glancing at her Bolivia watch, "Does he think our roots are in *Genesis* and that's why the Southern Baptists apologized for supporting racism and asked for forgiveness?"

"You mean the over fifteen-million predominately White Southern Baptists that met in Atlanta, Georgia this past June?"

"Yea...at their National Convention in the Declaration of Repentance and Rededication regarding racial reconciliation. Well, let's say they've a handful of Blacks including our church."

Sally, herself a Baptist, spoke of how the Southern Baptist Convention asked forgiveness for condoning racism for most of its 150-year history, and how its president said it has more work to be done in its 15.6 million-member church...the nation's largest Protestant denomination. She said that the denomination failed to support the civil rights movement of the 1950s and Sixties, and that it was in 1989 when the denomination first declared racism a sin.

"At the June convention they denounced racism in all its

forms as deplorable sin," Sally continued. "And girlfriend, the apology resolution was approved overwhelmingly by over 20,000 convention members."

"I thought it was a courageous move that deserves the Nobel Peace Prize. Especially when their resolution stated: 'We lament and repudiate historic acts of evil such as slavery from which we continue to reap a bitter harvest, and we recognize that the racism which yet plagues our culture today is inextricably tied to the past."

"Girlfriend, you must have memorized the whole resolution, didn't you?"

"Just excerpts from it because the whole idea was such a courageous move that took tremendous humility! But as usual, no one was paying very much attention with their fragile egos."

"That's right. You should know all about it 'cause you had to write about it in *The Miami Times*. Mr. Hamuludin had you do the research and submit articles and follow-ups on that subject."

"I enjoyed it, Sally. The resolution even stated this: 'We apologize to African Americans for condoning...or perpetuating individual and systematic racism in our lifetime. We ask for forgiveness from our African American brothers and sisters, acknowledging that our own healing is at stake; and we hereby commit ourselves to eradicate racism in all its forms from Southern Baptist life and ministry.'"

Sally stared hard at me and shook her head. "You really took that apology seriously, didn't you? You sound like a professional orator!"

"Can you think of any move more courageous and touching than the move they made? Sally, it takes strong personalities for Whitefolks to stand up and speak out with that kind of courage!"

"Alice Johnson, you and I talked about this a few months ago, didn't we? And I told you that to merely denounce historical racism and slavery and not seeking to promote justice and equality in today's society is useless. Just look at this Simpson case!"

"And I told you this courageous apology from Southern

Baptists leaders should have made history and dominated the news media all over the world instead of the *People vs Simpson* case. We need to build moral and spiritual values in our children."

"Well, girlfriend, you can help build moral and spiritual values in our children by baking some of your good brownies for my youth group bake sale we're having this Sunday at Second Baptist."

"I might just do that; and I'll also tell your predominately Black youth group to add the names of those courageous White men who wrote that resolution to their list of positive role models, and join them in their pursuit. Our youth are our leaders of tomorrow."

"I agree. Those White men are positive role models." Then staring at the thin, Caucasian bag lady that frequents a crossroad near the park, she added, "I heard you sometimes give her brownies, too. So, bake enough for her, 'cause if Simpson's found guilty, the shock could turn you into a bag-lady yourself since you seem so depressed about the trial and the racial division it could be causing. Even in her predicament, that White homeless bag lady feels far more important than you and me. And probably she even feels that she's far more important than O.J!"

Feeling heavy hearted, I made the sign of the cross. "If she feels that way it's because of programmed White supremacy, Sally. It's not her fault if she feels more important than Blacks. We have to blame those adults who taught her this as a child. Besides, her present behavior as a bag lady could be the result of her being a battered wife."

"Even so, she probably still feels superior just as some Whitefolks like that Los Angeles policeman Mark Fuhrman who is the main witness for the prosecution in the Simpson trial."

"That's programmed hatred. It surprised me when he said he hadn't used the word 'nigger' in the last ten years."

"Didn't you hear those sickening tape-recorded conversations?" she asked above the happy laughter of multi-ethnic children hurrying toward the Coral Reef School playground.

"Didn't you hear all that racist and sexist venom?" .

"Let's not even talk about the taped-conversations," I suggested as we continued in step. "Programmed white supremacy begins in the innocence of childhood. Grown-ups teach it." Every so often I would pause for a few seconds and feed the ducks. "Violence begins in childhood."

But Sally was determined to express her anger. "Fuhrman even spoke of genocide and said that if he had his way, he would take all the niggers, put them together in a big group and burn them!" She implied that racists like Fuhrman are fighting angry because Blackfolks like O.J. have betrayed the state of inferiority and submission that Whitefolks have assigned to them. "Girlfriend, the whole damn issue is about race and sex! That's why lots of Blackfolks feel that White racists policeman framed him. Most White women don't see this. You see, girlfriend, money is the controlling factor! Money!"

Maybe I haven't the intelligence to see it either because I'm focused on wife abuse and that doesn't come in a color, I thought to myself. I understood why some Black men feel that "as a Black man, success is marrying a White girl."

Sally continued talking about Fuhrman's taped-conversation to Laura Hart McKinny, a screenwriter, who at one time had been working on a script about the conflict between male and female police officers inside the Los Angeles Police Department. In the taped-conversation we heard Fuhrman spewing out hatred and filth. What was depressingly disturbing to Sally was the uncaring concern of our White Christian community who ignored the taped-conversation and who refuse to believe that racism permeates our society.

I too, found this very disturbing and depressing. My mind was in no mood to further discuss that kind of programmed hate and I asked the universe to please do something.

(Later I would learn that "the word 'nigger' passed from Fuhrman's lips as naturally as breath." I learned of the taped-conversation in which Fuhrman spoke of people suspected of crimes being beaten to pulp by him; of the way he tortured suspects, forcing them to confess; of him planting evidence that would make the suspect appear guilty; of racial harassment, and of cases fabricated. His taped-conversation spoke of his disgust with interracial relationships; there were accounts of vicious slurs against Latinos, women, and gays. He boasted of his importance to the Simpson's prosecution and stated bluntly: "I'm the key witness in the trial of the century. If I go down, the glove goes out, and their case goes bye-bye").

Sally continued. "And it's all about money and sex 'cause it's right there in the Bible that's filled with the talk of money, sex and violence. White males dominate the Bible and it seems when they spoke of blessings, they always consisted of lots of money, lots of wives and children, and fighting bloody wars and winning. Look at Job. Look at how he was blessed with all that money after going through years of physical sickness and suffering. The Lord even blessed him with a brand new wife and lots of brand new kids."

"What kinds of messages are we getting here?" I was beginning to feel somewhat uncomfortable and confused.

Undoubtedly Sally, too, was beginning to feel very uncomfortable with the conversation because she paused and began laughing hysterically. Her hearty laughter triggered my snickering when I tried to ask her why was she laughing so hard. I paused again to throw bread crumbs to a gathering of ducks.

"Girlfriend," she said, still bellowing as she pointed to one white mallard duck chasing another. "Let's face it. Speaking of sex...Mother Nature is a sexy little witch! Everything she made is sexy, Alice. I know its for reproductive purposes, but Mother Nature made man the only species to use it for pleasure and to reproduce. That's how Adam and Eve got us into all this confusion. It's no wonder Tina Turner song "What's Love Got To Do With It" makes a lot of darn sense to some folks. According to the animals, it seems love has nothing to do with it. It's natural instinct for reproduction purposes. I wonder is it pleasurable to them? The way that female duck's running from that male duck, we humans would call that rape unless it's a game ducks play."

"It had better be a game they play. Mother Nature gave us humans a double blessing, so what are you trying to say, Sally?" I asked, now skipping every so often to keep up with her fast-paced walking.

Still laughing she replied, "But, like you said... every blessing is a potential curse. I guess we've gotta admit that there's something about the pleasure of sex that controls people, and often times it triggers violence in men...uncontrollable violence. Animals don't kill for sex... but male humans do. They abuse it."

"That's why reciprocal love has everything to do with it."

"Even so, its an awfully powerful feeling Mother Nature created in man. And then Adam and Eve gets cursed for what Nature did. It's no wonder some of these poor ol' innocent priests sometimes find it awfully difficult to be celibate in spite of their dedication to God."

"Aristotle said there are two peak pleasures: thinking and sex."

"Mother Nature makes you frigid if you're thinking while having sex. She makes you stay focused if you want to enjoy it. 'Stay focus, don't think, kept those hands moving, lose control.'"

"That sounds like the same behavior required for creative writing."

Sally paused to massage her right hipbone. "Then if you want to go solo, she eventually gives you muscle strain or arthritis to cramp your style."

I frowned. "What does muscle strain or arthritis have to do with it?"

Ignoring my question, Sally continued: "Writing is thinking. Religious ministers are devoted to thinking and that's supposed to be their peak pleasure."

"What a blessing and a sacrifice."

"It's a mission without their permission, girlfriend. I'm

beginning to question this blessing we call free will."

I smiled, then jumped from the path of a group of oncoming skaters. "Mother Nature has made enjoying sex a blessing and a curse. More of a curse than a blessing nowadays because of the HIV virus."

Sally agreed. "My doctor said he was checking one of his male patients and asked has he ever had any bad sex ..meaning did the patient ever have sex with someone who had a venereal disease. The patient knew exactly what the doctor had reference to and said, 'Yes!" Then, the doctor asked, 'How was it?' And the patient lit up and said, 'It sure was goo-o-o-o-o-o-d!'"

Again, we laughed heartily, breaking our walking-beat as we stumbled down the path, laughing and holding our stomachs.

"Girlfriend," she said through chuckling breaths, "It's just like your husband's colleague told you and John, 'If the Good Lord made anything that feels better than good sex, he must have kept it up in heaven with 'em. It's no wonder folks are dying to get there! Some even follow dominant, charismatic leaders to their deaths.'"

"People are dying to stop the violence so that we can get to the heaven that's within us, Sally." Suddenly, a light flashed on inside my higher consciousness and I saw the entire picture that love is the great motive. But then I felt that I would be unable to clearly explain what was being revealed.

Feeling an urgent need to at least attempt to explain the revelation, I said, "Jesus said the kingdom of heaven is within us. But we only get there through our unconditional love for one another. We first have to believe this. When a man and wife love each other unconditionally, they have the golden keys to open those gates that lead into the kingdom of heaven..to enjoy each other sexually and otherwise in their united companionship. Mother Nature has taught us that love finds expression through kindness and concern. Mother Nature also teaches us that fear...known as hate...destroys love. When we disobey the universal laws of cause and effect, we're punished, that is, we do not enter the kingdom of heaven that's already within ourselves. When we don't love, we live, move and have our being in darkness. Whereas, on the other hand, when we love, we live, move and have our being in a heaven-like atmosphere! Nature never forgives when we disobey her! When you hate, you deny feeling love. When you feel love, you are entering the kingdom of heaven within yourself for it is the highest excitement."

Sally chuckled. "Girlfriend, I hear what you're saying and to me, it makes a whole lot of sense. But to these folks who believe in all this crazy violence and hate, it's much ado about nothing. Maybe we oughta put it into their language and tell them that heaven is the big orgasm. I bet they'll straighten up and start treating other folks as they themselves wish to be treated so they can get there!"

"That's exactly what one of my creative writing professor once said heaven is. And I thought he was being vulgar."

"God didn't create anything vulgar. Man attaches definitions to experiences. That kind of awareness by your creative writing professor comes from deep insight,.. evaluations."

"The Trial of the Century requires deep insight, evaluations. There're lots of lessons to be learned from it. To us, the Juice seemed to be Mother Nature's favorite child, and probably still is 'cause he's being used as a kind of sacrifice to help us awaken to Nature's gift to us all and which we are abusing. The Juice had a beautiful wife whom he loved dearly and who loved him, he even had wealth and fame! He even had loads of love for everybody, and everybody loved him, just like everybody loves Oprah."

Gesturing with my hands as we continued walking, I cleared my throat and continued: "It seems the love he had for his beautiful wife, like most of us have for our spouses, was conditional. Mother Nature wants it to be unconditional...totally unselfish... if we are to enter that joy known as the kingdom of heaven which we all already possess; and if we are to enjoy the companionship of one another and our material possessions with which we are blessed."

Then smiling, I began singing: "'The greatest thing you'll ever learn is just to love and be loved in return.'"

Sally clasped her palms together. "Especially the man and wife who has experienced the highest peak of excitement, then abuse it by letting fear, hate jealousy, control, anger, impatience, selfishness destroy their unconditional love for each other."

"I think that's what *Genesis* is trying to tell us when it spoke of Adam and Eve. Whoever retranslated the story sorta got the idea goofed up."

Sally disagreed, "It all depends on who's doing the interpreting. Just as you stated in your book, it doesn't matter how intelligent a person is, what he's saying can only be understood in proportion to the intelligence of the person listening to it. The same principal applies in listening to the Simpson case. You've gotta find the message that's there for you!"

I snatched a green leaf from the black olive tree as we passed. "And, Sally, by using my therapy, I'm able to understand much of the spiritual message, only because I truly believe that we're all evolving as we continue on a spiritual journey to the kingdom of heaven that's within us all. And that we're spirits within the mind of our Creator."

Sally nodded. "It takes a lot of faith to reach that level of thinking."

"It's the grace of the Creator that reveals it to you through deep meditation when you ask in the midst of pain and suffering. That's why thinking is a peak pleasure. The Creator is Mind."

Stretching her arms in midair for more exercise as we continued walking, Sally smiled and asked, "Didn't you say it was your analyst who told you not to deny yourself the joy of loving other people when you were having problems getting along with your co-workers at the university?"

"I most certainly did tell you that years ago, Sally. Why?"

She chuckled. "It's just strange that Whitefolks would say a thing like that when most of them don't like people of color. And, girlfriend, the Simpson case is showing it like it is. We all know that this racial hatred has gotta stop. I'm beginning to understand why the Southern Baptists Convention made that resolution. This thing has to start somewhere; and they had the guts to speak out."

"I told you -u-u-u-u. Do you think religion's the answer?"

"Religion is personal," she said and shrugged. "And I'm sure no White or Black person in his right mind is gonna let hating people keep him from entering that kingdom of heaven that's within him, just as Jesus has taught ages ago. That's why I can't understand how anyone could sprew out all that venom on those tapes. Why does a handsome and intelligent man like him need to hold on to an attitude of White supremacy? Damn!"

Understanding that White supremacy has programmed too many White people, despite their condition and status, to feel more important than Blacks and people of color, I saw no need to further discuss the problem of racism. Instead, we needed to begin doing something as a people to help each other return to love..unconditional love. We need to overwhelmingly support the predominately Southern Baptist Convention with its over eight million followers.

With this thought, I told Sally that it is our mission to help one another, then quoted: "See yourself in others. Whom can you hurt?"

"Well it seems someone has hurt that poor little bag lady parked on the ground over there," she said, as we again passed by her and waved.

Seeing myself in the homeless lady, I made the sign of the cross and said: "Sally, we don't understand many things; that's why we've gotta keep growing spiritually."

"Well, they said most poor folks are always spiritual. Living in poverty sorta makes you that way. So don't come telling me that suffering is a gift 'cause I'll kick your behind. Money has healing power!"

"But love has the greatest healing power," I recounted, feeling strangely touched by the tranquil lady. Wondering about choices and why did Mother Nature create the peaceful looking bag lady and the homeless in all races, colors and nationalities, I wanted to ask the universe was I destined to be a bag lady, and would it be its choice or mine? The trial of the century had led me to question free will. When I told Sally this, she questioned the theory and suggested we leave Mother Nature and her hidden agenda alone.

"I've gotten too old to be worrying about Mother Nature," she said, now complaining about her arthritis and suggesting that we end the walk.

"But there's joy in aging. You can no longer say that you're too young for Medicare and to old for the men to care."

Sally giggled. "You're darn right, girlfriend, 'cause I've become a frivolous old gal. I'm seeing five devoted gentlemen every day. As soon as I awake, *Will Power* helps me outta bed. When he leaves, I go visit *John*. Then *Charley Horse* comes along and when he's here, he takes a lot of my attention. When he leaves, *Arthur Ritis* shows up and stays the rest of the day. He doesn't like to stay in one place very long so he takes me from joint to joint. After such a busy day, I'm really tired and ready to go to bed with *Ben Gay*."

We both laughed and Sally continued: " My granddaughter said "Grandma, you're always thinking about sex; you oughta be thinking about the hereafter.' I told her 'honey, I'm always thinking about the hereafter. Every time I go to the garage to get something and I forget what it is that I'm supposed to be getting, I stop and ask, 'Lord, what am I here after?'"

We laughed so hard, we folded into the open arms of Charley Horse, unaware that months later domestic violence would claim Sally's life.

The next day when I anxiously visited my husband at the VA Medical Center and we sat on the westside patio chatting, I told him what Sally had said about the loving church Blackfolks giving wealthy O.J. God's ten-percent when the Good Lord has a difficult time collecting it from them Himself, he folded in laughter.

We had just come from Sunday Morning mass, which was held in the beautiful VAMC chapel. The medical center that sprawled two square blocks was surrounded by two huge hospitals, namely: The University of Miami/Jackson Memorial and Cedars that seemed to comprise a whole city within a city, populated by thousands of workers (whom we called God's earthly angels) and patients combined. And because the hospitals comprised a city within a city, John and I named this metropolis "The City Where Love is Multicultural."

Staring at John, I snickered into his continued laughter, adding more fuel to it. "Poor church folks giving rich O. J. their dimes."

"The people who gave O.J. the money gave it from their heart, Alice," he said, removing his eyeglasses and scratching into his neatly trimmed salt & pepper hair. "The heart is the center of our intelligence."

I gulped. "The other day you referred to the heart as a computer, and that a total understanding of all things can only come from your heart. From where did you get all this wise information, John?"

"Solitude, Alice."

"So solitude gives us 'heart intelligence' because it's the heart that speaks to us, not our minds?" I adjusted his navy necktie.

He smiled and nodded his head. "The mind should always listen to the heart, Alice."

"Then it's the heart with all it's intelligence that speaks out against domestic violence because the heart is love, just as Sally said."

"Sally's smart."

We talked about Sally and her jealous boyfriend, Frederick. I told him that Sally said she knew Simpson and his family when she taught at Galileo High School in San Francisco. We talked about the trials and agreed that the universe is sending us violent children a message from the heart to love one another with our hearts.

Squeezing John's hand, I chuckled and continued, "Besides, Sally said who else could better call to world attention the seriousness of wife abuse and violence than this mysterious O.J. the universe created. She said sometimes in his angry rage, her jealous Fred threatens her with his 'One of these days, I'm gonna do the O.J. on you!' control tactic."

John frowned. "Wow! If he feels that way, she'd better leave that cat alone!"

"She loves 'im, John; especially all those apartment buildings he owns. The guy's wealthy! He's Latin-American and has silky hair. But she hates his jealous behavior. You used to scare hell outta me with your jealous behavior...and we both survived."

"Oh boy! Thanks to the analyst."

I agreed, adding our gratitude to our family physician, Dr. McAdory, and our church ministers for also keeping us from losing control of our anger in the midst of overwhelming frustrations and raging arguments. "It takes a village to save a marriage from domestic violence," I chirped, then began talking emotionally about the Simpson trials and the excessive stress of awaiting the verdict. (Because of the hundred-thousand earthly angel-employees that are attending the sick, let me confess that we borrowed the phrase "Where love is international" from our Christ the King Catholic Church in South Dade).

He stared at me, adjusted his glasses and smiled. "Peace."

But I was far removed from any feelings of peace.

John suggested that I let the jury handle that, and counseled that I trust the jury system. I told him that Black jurors were less likely to believe the police version of things than White jurors. He agreed with me that this was mainly because Black jurors are more likely to have been victimized, or know someone who has been victimized by police misconduct.

I wanted to talk about the racial climate that the Simpson trial was triggering.

But my husband didn't want to talk about the racial climate or the taped conversation, he wanted to talk about O.J. BC (O.J. Before the Charges), not O.J. AD (America's Divide). He has always enjoyed talking about Simpson. and how he is one of the greatest athletes in college and professional football history. He said that Simpson was a student at the University of Southern California around the same time when Martin Luther King died, and that he was named an All American and won the 1968 Heisman Trophy. He talked about the time when Simpson was named NFL most valuable player for 1975, the year after we moved to Miami and the same year I returned to graduate school to earn the doctorate and left him alone at home with his disability... labeling it a form of husband abuse. He talked about how O.J. was inducted in the Football Hall of Fame in 1985, the year Grandma died while living with us. She, too, was an ardent O.J. fan. I was an ardent fan because he was such a mystery! I wondered was this his hundredth life back to planet earth and did he forget his mission like most of us who are searching for life's understanding.

My John has always been a sports addict. He himself played high school and college baseball. In 1954, after returning from the Korean War and playing baseball with winning Gimlet softballers, he was asked to join the Cincinnati Reds field team but his mother objected because of her concern for his mysterious stumbling prior to being diagnosed with MS. He could hit homeruns like Willie Mays, but this was due to his exceptionally keen vision which was later impaired by MS. So much for Mother Nature and her hidden agendas.

Knowing that my John has faith in the American judicial system, I did not introduce my fears that the Simpson cases were sending us a most disturbing message that race overshadows all logical reasoning. In the appeal to reason, Baruch Spinoza considered the intellectual love of God the highest good man can attain. I was now wondering where does this fit into the racial equation that was now exploding before us while we lingered in the state of denial.

Many African Americans like myself were worried that the Los Angeles Police Department and the media were making a mockery of justice in America. "The racial climate seems to color and influence everything we do on a societal level," many had voiced, recalling examples from the Civil Rights Movement in which many of us were sent to jail, beaten and/or killed for peacefully demonstrating while the White churches stood on the sidelines silently watching.

Following the Civil Rights Movement and after moving to Miami, John and I became advocates of multicultural education and began writing a series of musicals under the umbrella of "Keepers of the Dream." So successful were we into this annual project, *The Miami Herald* had labeled us "Playwrights for the Children" and had written a number of articles about our writing spree, implying that John and I were becoming legends. The Black weekly newspaper, *The Miami Times*, had introduced us to the Miami community the second year we arrived from Cincinnati, Ohio, because we were such advocates of multicultural education. Even television joined in, projecting our new-found talents and presenting our first musical docudrama, *Harriet Tubman in Narrative Song and Dance*, on educational TV- Channel 17 for almost eight years. We had written a musical docudrama based on writer Alex Haley's bestseller *Roots* entitled *Haley's Comet* which was scheduled to be produced as a tribute to the now deceased author, but my obsession with the Simpson Case pushed that project on the back burner.

CHAPTER THREE

Lord, when doubts fill my mind, when my heart is in turmoil, quiet me and give me renewed hope and cheer. Will you permit a corrupt government to rule under your protection...a government permitting wrong to defeat right? - Psalms 94: 19-20

"O.J. Simpson's case pushed a myriad of projects on the back burner," I said to the universe after hearing news reports that the buzzer form the jury room had sounded three times to indicate that a verdict had been reached in the criminal trial. It was the following morning when the jury's sealed verdict was handed to Judge Ito to read.

On October 3, 1995 the long criminal trial ended with Simpson's acquittal on charges of murder. Never before had I experienced so much buried anger and division in our beautiful nation that has even withstood the ugliness of American slavery and the bloody trails of the Civil Rights Movement. Most Whites still felt strongly that Simpson was guilty of the double murders and they were furious that he was found not guilty. Most Blacks who always believed that Simpson was innocent of the double murders and felt he had been framed, applauded his acquittal because..to quote an except from Psalm 94, they did not "approve of those who condemn the innocent to death." They prayed that the justice system would continue its search to find out who did this senseless, brutal killing of two innocent people, and why? There were too many unanswered questions that left us puzzled, for instance, we could not understand how could O.J. brutally kill two people in the time frame given when one of the victims vigorously fought back and was stabbed several times. There were no body bruises on O.J? How do we explain the absence of a huge amount of blood? In my opinion, there were fifteen or more seeds of reasonable doubts that he committed the murders.

The attacks leveled against the fourteen-member jury by those who felt Simpson guilty were very disturbing. While all our views were shaped by what we saw on TV, read in the newspapers, tabloids, magazines; heard on TV talk shows, on radio panels, we were in no position to mock the jury's verdict.

Listening to the intelligence of my heart, I could clearly see that the Simpson case did not cause the racial divide but it did prove to us all again that the problem of the twenty-First Century is the problem of the color line. While it is true that psychology endeavors to understand the conscious and subconscious forces that instill and motivate behavior, I found that very little research has been done to understand racism.

"So this is the universal message of the case?" I said to the universe, rejoicing that my heart had now found the answer. Immediately, I continued my spiritual mission to help promote racial harmony in the world. (Note: 18 months later the national news reported that four South Carolina churches (Lutheran, Anglican, Roman Catholic and United Methodist) "confessed to the 'sin of racism'... the powerful prejudice which pits one race against the other to the damage of all," and asked the Creator for forgiveness). The Simpson case, a blessing in disguise, was bringing racism to the forefront.

Suddenly, while I was engrossed in helping to promote racial harmony, an act of domestic violence blew my world into shreds and I fell to my knees crying for help! Why? Because although I was shocked that Sally's life was snatched away that June of 1996 due to a diabetic coma, I learned six months later that her beloved Fred had beaten her to death. Sally had remarried her ex-husband,

Isaac Nkumbula who had left his second wife to remarry Sally, and according to Isaac, Fred exploded in anger, beating her mercilessly the night before she died in the diabetic coma. Her diabetes and the beatings were well kept secrets by Sally; and Isaac, himself plagued with terminal cancer, begged me to let the issues lay to rest, otherwise, Fred would begin stalking me and it was too dangerous.

Why? Because according to Isaac, Fred blamed John and me for the breakup, citing that we put the scare in Sally about his hostile attitude. He also blamed our book, *Mysterious Stranger Aboard*, which gave Sally the "stupid" idea of forgiving, re-marrying and caring for her disabled husband and father of her children because she still loved and respected him.

Undoubtedly I went into shock, confused and angry, realizing that the universe had made the Simpson trial a blessing and a curse (cross). My heart was heavy with pain because my best friend, Sally, was a fatal victim of domestic abuse. It seemed I couldn't stop weeping. Sally's loving personality of kindness and concern reminded me so much of Patty's.

To add to my state of shock and confusion, the news media blasted with a report of the 39-year-old Laotian immigrant who lives in Daytona Beach, Florida and who, a few days earlier, murdered his 23-year old wife, their three daughters, ages 2, 4, and 7 and his 61-year-old mother-in-law. His lawyer said the Laotian went amok because he was jealous of his wife's success as a businesswoman.

Wrestling with mounting confusions, I ran to my analyst's office crying for help, asking why was the universe giving us the O.J. Simpson and company courses in human behavior?

"Use your therapy to cope with the experiences," my analyst counseled. "Man needs difficulties; they're necessary for health."

"Spiritual and physical health," I said and groaned, overly concerned about the amount of excessive stress we children of the universe were undergoing.

When I groaned, he stated that my only concern, now, is how to handle an excessive amount of difficulties that John and I were creating from the Simpson case. He strongly suggested that I let Sally's spirit rest, because I didn't need her boyfriend stalking me nor visiting my disabled husband at the hospital. He suggested that I leave Sally's world out of my world and concentrate on John until I can fully regain intellectual control of my own thoughts and feelings that speak from the depths of the heart.

"That's preposterous!" I had said, knowing that he had reference to my writing. Feeling grateful for his counseling, I decided to follow his advice because I feared and hated Fred's violent wrath. Even though I longed to write about Sally in collaboration with her daughter who had said Fred threatened "to do the O.J." on her loving mother and he did it and was getting away with it, I felt the strong urge to follow my analyst's professional warning. He had suggested that as a tribute to Sally and without using her name, I could write on the subject of domestic violence to let the healing begin.

I agreed. Besides, I wanted to free myself of being obsessed with the Simpson trials, return to reality and create from an alternative world of related experiences in which life's message is the same. Love!

At this point, feeling agitated, disturbed, and angry, I stopped reading the manuscript, laid it aside and began pacing my home office floor. I stared at the computer then at the wall clock. It was still early morning and I felt the need to write through my writer's block as a healing process in spite of echoes from the Simpson trial now breaking through the six-o'clock morning news.

I wanted to write away all the mountains of frustrations and focus in on symbols of love. And, according to the universe...since love is the only answer, what then is the question?

The question is why a civil trial?

2

Happy is the man that findeth wisdom, and the man that getteth understanding - The Bible, Proverbs 29:18
January, 1997

Despite the unanimous decision of the jury in the criminal trial, Americans, predominately White, continued to debate over whether Simpson committed the murders. Most African Americans felt that the reaction to the not guilty verdict demonstrated the intensity of America's race problem, especially when we wondered why did the case have such an emotional impact on Whites? Aren't we on planet earth to spread love?

What really sent me into a stage of deep depression was the racist-like viciousness in reaction to the civil trial "not guilty" verdict. The news media seemed to be condemning the predominately African-American and female jury of twelve ..including three Whites and two men. The news media reflected the thoughts and feelings of most Whites.

Observing all this, I was led to believe that White America was questioning the jury's intellectual ability to deal with the scientific evidence provided by the prosecution. Repeatedly, I asked the universe what was the motivation behind the civil case in which the murdered victims families and most White Americans wanted to find Simpson liable?

As the Civil trial moved forward with a predominately White jury this time, the procedures demonstrated how the mental state of racism serves to impair the ability to reason. Therapy had taught me that once the ability to reason is impaired, the emotions are allowed to dominate and control our behavior. Whether we do what we do necessarily or contingently, we are nevertheless led by hope and fear. Man act out of fatalistic necessity according to this nature. It is only love and magnanimity that we can overcome the resistance of those who are offended by our reasonings. We all live for the pursuit of greater understanding, inasmuch as we know that there is only one world...it is the world of thinking and extended substance which we often refer to as God or love.

While tensely awaiting the verdict of the civil trial, I wanted to write about Sally but decided to write about Patty whose spirit, mysteriously, became synonymous with Sally's and other battered women.

The computer and I became the best of friends, and now I was ready to write into my writer's block as I stationed myself in our home-base office, waiting.

Swept into a compelling force to examine these questions, I decided to consider an alternative route by focusing Patty's universal message that love is expressed through kindness and concern. I re-entered my literary world of solitude to let the spirits speak. Because my restless mind kept focusing the Simpson trials and Patty whose unconditional love was felt and remembered by those who knew and loved her, I relaxed, easing into a mystic state to record the message.

In every experience there is a message of love to be learned, practiced or exemplified. Patty's life was a message. And when she died, many of us died with her instead of living her message and lighting up the world on our journey together. This same experience holds true for today's victims whose lives we are now grieving. Why can't I write about our grief for them? Because it is far too painful. It brings back pain from the various chapters of early childhood.

Even as a grieving six-year-old who could not stop crying at Patty's funeral, I had profound feelings that she was a special angel, and my dreams often revealed this. And now, sixty-two years later, looking back into my childhood thoughts and feelings from an adult level of wisdom, knowledge and understanding, I can see that she indeed was an angel who had come into this world with an enlightened mind. She lived her message in those seventeen years; and then her mission was completed.

Heartbreakingly, I recall a childhood experience that follows me to this day. I remember that two years after Patty's funeral, I wrote about her spirit in an essay entitled "Dawn." Why? Because my older sister had said that one of the poems in American Literature that Patty religiously loved was William Cullen Bryant's "Thanatopsis," a beautiful poem about death in which Bryant gave his views of natural scenery. I read the poem repeatedly and became obsessed with nature. Swept into a world of beauty in which I felt at one with all creation, I wrote the essay "Dawn," depicting my deepest thoughts and feelings that embraced Patty's happy and peaceful journey into eternal life. Dawn. Throughout the writing, I recalled being in a state of solitude, and then completely mesmerized! So beautiful and peaceful was this state of mind...this state of oceanic tranquility... that I wanted to live in it forever...creating beauty that was already created to its highest perfection by the universe. I was watching God with God's eyes.

It has been said that for every blessing, there is a potential curse. Being an eight-year-old third-grader and writing an essay as a class assignment, I was not aware that sharing the essay would bring me so much pain. Here is what happened: The teacher called each of us students individually to come to the front of the class to read our essays. When it came my turn, I felt excited and humbly read the essay to a sea of beautiful, happy faces that the universe had created in its work of art. My classmates applauded and I smiled, easing back into my seat with feelings of love throughout the universe.

"Hold it, Alice Ward!" my teacher, whom I dearly loved and respected, said. She snatched the essay from my hand, then rereading it to the class and scornfully commenting on every line, she ripped it to shreds and pitched it in the wastebasket. She then turned and scolded me, shouting that I had stolen the material because no eight-year-old could write with so much wisdom and creativeness. The children folded in laughter, some rolling all over the floor, some bellowing so hard they had to run to the bathroom. The pain of my beautiful teacher's anger pierced my heart so badly that I folded in tears and decided to never write again. And I didn't. Nor did I want to think of Patty anymore, and undoubtedly her spirit stopped visiting me. In my world, life's beauty that Patty's spirit shared with me, had faded. I wept, dried my eyes and continued the journey as I moved through the darkness in my lifelong search for the brightest of lights into which I once walked. That kind of mental abuse was child abuse.

Because time is nature's universal cure for all ills, I had completely forgotten about the childhood incident. Then, approximately forty years after the African-American teacher ripped my essay to shreds, my Anglo-Saxon analyst, Dr. Kensinger, in 1975 flushed out the cobwebs of this long forgotten episode. How did this come about? It happened like this:

After my husband became totally disabled with multiple sclerosis, we retired from our school teaching positions and moved from Cincinnati, Ohio to Miami. He was the patient, I was his caregiver. Unable to cope with the sudden changes brought about by MS such as frustrations, depressions, exhaustion, anxiety, guilt, anger; and the loss of privacy, future plans, economic security, health, family, friends, and work, we both felt hopeless.

"Let's talk about it," my analyst suggested in his usual gentle voice.

My feelings of hopelessness escalated and tears began flowing from my eyes, I was too choked-up to talk and was wrestling with Anorexia and Bulemia.

He pulled a Kleenex from the box stationed on his mahogany desktop and handed it to me.

Jerking with tears, I still could not talk.

Aware of this, he counseled, "When you return home, find yourself a quiet space to meditate on what you're feeling. Write it down and bring it to me when you come to the next scheduled session. Then we can discuss it."

Following his counseling and engaging in periods of deep meditation, I wrote about my thoughts and feelings concerning John's illness and the frustrations we were encountering. At the next therapy session, I handed my analyst a copy of the assignment.

With stretched eyes, he silently read it. Suddenly he stared at me and said, "You're a writer!"

"What?" I was stunned by his response to my assignment. I expected him to comment on the thoughts and feelings that were hurting, not my writing.

"Tell me about your childhood writings," he said.

"I don't recall doing any serious writing in childhood other than my school assignments."

"Did any of your teachers comment on your ability to write creatively?"

"I've never written anything creatively. But strangely enough, when I was in college, I do recall my Master's Thesis advisors commenting on how well I documented the case studies I researched for my study."

"When you go home this afternoon, I suggest that you go back into deep meditation and see can you recall any writing experiences which you really enjoyed doing when you were a child."

Again, following his counseling, I went into deep meditation, but nothing about my childhood writing surfaced. I recalled making straight A's on written book reviews and other written reports that called for deep feelings from the heart when I was in undergrad and grad school. Often times the instructors used my reports as models, and they were often put on display. I was grateful and felt humble.

At the next therapy session, I told my analyst about the excellent grades I made on written book reports, and especially in large graduate classes at the University of Cincinnati in which I was the only African American. While chatting away, I suddenly recalled the childhood episode that snatched the light out off my life, I sat there, transfixed, telling my analyst about the experience and crying throughout the session.

There was the answer! It has been said that "Childhood is the playpen of adulthood!" And with this awakening, I resumed creative writing, bringing my husband along on the journey of expressing our thoughts and feelings in the healing process.

And now, Patty's spirit had resurfaced with the Simpson trial, urging me to speak out in behalf of abused women like myself, and like my own abused sister, Leather, who died at age twenty-one when I was ten-years-old. I spoke of Leather in our book, *Love Paints Beauty in the Soul*, and how she was abused by her husband. Leather and Patty were best friends and classmates in the eleventh grade when I was in the first.

Why was Patty's spirit revisiting and recreating within me so much depression? Oh, she's here to help me write!

African American ministers throughout Miami, and especially Reverend Walter Richardson of Sweet Home Missionary Baptist Church and Father Richard Barry of Saint Agnes Episcopal Church, said that the universe missioned Mr. Simpson to carry the cross that will bring us a spiritual message, and that only in quietness and solitude will we hear the universal message. I entered into solitude, and the message that kept focusing was that we all have a mission to love and help one another.

"Patty's was a life that challenged us to choose love instead of hate because hate triggers violence," my older sister had said. In childhood, I shared with Leather and Patty a common bond to help spread love. And now they're dictating the story!

Listening closely to the dictates of the soul, my busy fingers resumed moving across computer keys writing Patty's autobiography, my mind fighting to dismiss buried feelings of sadness and multifaceted experiences the news media was triggering again about the civil trial.

In the midst of agonizing frustrations and protagonists semblance of the battered women that kept moving through my mind, I continued typing, tearfully reminiscing a message Patty had lived in her enlightened world before her young spirit made its exit into eternity. Her departure now reminded me of the departure of the two loving spirits that pierce my thoughts. Therefore, to soften the pain that was continuously surfacing from the case which, for over two years, had disrupted my state of equilibrium, I needed to converse with Patty and company in spite of writer's block that might evade the flow. Somehow, I felt strongly that the wisdom learned from the experiences would be identical, and that the Creator is forever sending us repeated symbols of love to help us on this journey amid the calm and the strife.

While it is true that as Patty's devoted friends who felt that she came into this world with an enlightened mind, we needed to carry her message. In so doing, this would enable us to find unity and wholeness within ourselves at a time when the Simpson trial was challenging us to a lot of unanswered questions about our own prejudices and ungodliness, our own selfishness and fragile egos.

"Why not write about the messages which we're getting from the case?" my husband had whispered from his hospital bed as he courageously wrestled with multiple sclerosis and a serious bedsore that seemed to be taking ages to heal. I now wondered did his obsession with the trial have anything to do with the slow healing process of that sore. After all, it had been over a year when the ulcer was discovered, approximately in the midst of the criminal trial period that kept us all on edges.

In spite of the pain, I agreed to write about Patty as a symbol of love even amid the symbols of hate we experience in everyday life; especially the reports that come over the news media that keep us well informed of current events that make us happy, sad and indifferent. Somewhere among the love/hate messages of the past and present, we will meet with the messages of the future as we continue to evolve after exposing the violence we tend to cover-up for personal reasons.

Certainly I was anxious to write, knowing that writing is the mind/body medicine to which we had become addicted. Writing had, through years of endless pain and suffering with his mysterious stranger, enriched our knowledge and taught us that sorrow is the path to the soul. Yes, life's mysterious experiences, especially the Simpson drama, had shown us that sorrow is nature's device through which we human beings are conditioned to become cooperative and humble in human relationships.

Dauntlessly pulling the thoughts together and fitting them into the puzzle of writer's block that I sensed coming aboard, I continued typing, negotiating Plan Two and letting my thoughts weave in and out without interruption. Perhaps I was running out of fear that bouts of depression would intervene as they had done in past literary worlds for the past two years. But isn't this typical of all writers. Study after study has shown that people in the arts suffer disproportionately high rates of mood disorders, particularly manic depression and major depression, according to *The Miami Herald*.

It was still early morning...the time-space when the physical universe and I hold silent seminars. And because James Redfield's fictional work, *The Celestine Prophecy*, implied that the physical universe is pure energy, a higher source that will respond to what we think about it, I wanted to think that it is the epitome of intelligence and has all the answers the trial was seeking. I wanted to think that it would help Patty and all spirits of abused wives come forward and help us women speak out against this enemy called hate, because hate triggers violence. I wanted to believe that the universe would help us understand the case and who's actually playing the race card, and was our secretive wife-abusive hero framed?

Episodes of the spiritual-based manuscript continued flowing as I typed, seemingly uninterrupted, eager to share the soul-stirring epitaph with its roots of love in the book of *Genesis*. In my enlightened world, writing had become a form of "Centering Prayer"...a prayer that comes from the heart. It is a way of emptying the mind and imagination so that the Creator could fill it with His love....love that expresses itself through kindness and concern, and which I needed at this time.

Every so often, visions of Patty's smile would flash into the stillness, alighting the pages that were relating her vigorous message which we all needed to help us survive life's turbulent journey. The inspirational hymn, *Lead On, O King Eternal,* by Ernest Warburton Shurtleff and Henry Smart which she loved according my older sister, flowed softly through my mind above the sound of commentaries coming from the home-based office intercom. It was a song that I had learned in childhood. The words, at that time, were just as powerful to my young mind as they are now to my adult understanding. Especially at a time when racism was showing its ugly face. Far above this face of racism was the brightest of lights ...a beautiful face of a former beauty queen, wife and mother shining through the TV courtroom screen and sending a message of love...a wake-up call to women... into a suffering world of darkness.

Thinking about abused women, my mind kept focusing Patty and the various responses made by those who loved her. I paused to reflect on what my older sister, Jessye, had earlier this week told me about Patty's eulogy.

"And, Alice the minister had said 'Hers was a message to help heal the world of man's inhumanity to man so that we can experience the beauty of life even amid adversities.'" She said the minister had solemnly eulogized that "To experience love in ourselves and in others is the meaning of life! We came here to co-create with God by extending love!"

For not with swords loud clashing nor roll or stirring drums,
But deeds of love and mercy the heavenly kingdom comes.

"It's a message which we all know to be a basic truth but cannot be found without great effort because 'all things excellent are as difficult as they are rare,'" I whispered, aggrieved, as anxious fingers now moved across computer keys. Yet, in my flight from bouts of depression that were beginning to gnaw at me because of unending sorrow and confusion stemming from The Case of the Century, I was determined to write the story regardless of the spiritual semblance of the deceased victims that kept intercepting and for good reason because it was a "wake-up" call from their spirits.

The song in my heart continued: *Lead on, O' King Eternal, we follow not with fear...*

"Patty's life was rare because it's still awakening us to question our own understandings in search for order, unity, wholeness; and eventually rise, too, to an enlightened mind, enabling us to also taste and see," I said into the soft sound of quietude. "Yes, her life was rare because it told us that all beings are already enlightened; it is only because of our delusions that we don't realize this!"

For gladness breaks like morning where'er Thy face appear...

With undiminished emotional intensity in search for The Holy Grail, I was burning to realize this and awaken to the miracle that is within us all. Ever since childhood, I had always been interested in the Arthurian legends; and now it all was beginning to light up that even spiritually, childhood is the playpen of adulthood.

Thy cross is lifted o'er us, we journey in its light...

Again, my thoughts lingered on the 17-year old spirit that had come and left her message like so many others are yet doing. And because the message still has roots in today's society that should be taught in early childhood, the pain is tender and long lasting because we are losing our children. How? They are killing up each other; they see grown ups doing it.. Most violent children come from the home of violent parents.

Still bereaved that violence is taking over our country and we seem to be in a state of helplessness, I kept begging the universe for answers that would help clean up the mess we keep making.

The crown awaits the conquest, lead on, O God of might!

The idea that the Creator is both cause and effect is something we should all think about. Considering the case, we are aware that we can only speak of our experiences in relation to our understanding, and not in relation to the Creator's, not to mention The Trial of the Century that is confusing us all. Inasmuch as we know, as Baruch Spinoza had said, that "it would assume a great imperfection in the Creator if anything happened against His will, or if His nature was so limited that, like us creatures, He had sympathy for some things and antipathy for others"...it would be completely opposed to the nature of the Creator's will.

But Spinoza was also into *Genesis*; and perhaps we needed to move back into the pages of biblical history and use Patty's light to help us understand and appreciate the message it is teaching.

"She's gone?..But she was such a saintly role model!" We continued to mourn, although aware that often times these are the spirits that come and go in the twinkling of an eye.

While my mind was moving into a state of depression, I thought about my loving twelve-year-old grandnephew, Tavis, who, only two years ago, had died due to an automobile accident while the faithful religious family was enroute to visit other family members. I thought about his youngest sister, my loving nineteen-year-old grandniece, Toinette, who, just one week ago, was driving to visit a dear classmate when her car collided with a truck and she was instantly killed. Those two little angels had left this world in the twinkling of an eye. I still was in silent tears, often mourning into the stillness.

So many young deaths of so many saint-like loved ones.

My thoughts again returned to Patty and our tearful inquires.

"But why did he have to kill her? Hate is a mean old disease. Perhaps the demise is a wake-up call for both spiritual and physical enlightenment, I thought to myself, typing into the humming of the air conditioning unit, my mind still moving into past conversations. I was using Patty's light along with that of other victims to help me see clearer the phases of human behavior, especially original man.

It was said that in the second time around, Simpson faced off against a dream team of lawyers who focused on his motives and received help from his so called old faithful friends, a myriad of new evidences and a pair of size 12-Bruno Magli shoes. It was said that the shoes would be the single most important piece of evidence in the case now had a predominately White jury. The civil defense lawyers stated that because the shoes had nothing to do with the Los Angeles Police Department, the shoes had nothing to do with race. Simpson had denied he owned the Bruno Maglis, and had given a conflicting version of his relationship with his wife, where he was the night of June 12, 1994 and how he cut his hand.

To many African Americans, the civil case seemed such a farce, but we were advised to listen and observe, even if it were synonymous to a daytime soap opera.

But listening to and observing the Simpson trial is *another world* to many of us because the stress could land us in *general hospital*, especially those activists ...*the young and the restless*..who will probably be the hip-hop generation *all the days of our lives* because in their rap lyrics they need the Creator's *guiding light as the world turns* from violence to nonviolence and we continue to evolve as a unified people, which would certainly be *the bold and the beautiful thing* to do at a time when race relations are being put to a serious test just as I've told *all my children*; and that our ministers told us that everyone should judge for himself what is offered to his mind because we only have *one life to live*, and that controversial issues like *The People vs Simpson* are the growth points of civilization.

3

"Civilization is fighting for its very life; all the seemingly little indulgences multiplied a millionfold may become the decisive factor in its survival."

"As civil rights advocates, let's continue to ease life's hurts by writing," my husband counseled from his hospital bed the following day when I visited him, telling him that the civil jury had heard the Simpson case and was now deliberating. This, alone was making me nervous.

Sitting by his bedside and combing his neatly trimmed hair,

we talked about the therapeutic practice of writing our thoughts and feelings about the case. He was implying that we had become writing addicts. On the other hand writing was a form of silent prayer from the depths of the hearts. His chronic illness had led us into this spiritual light.

I had stopped by the VA hospital to visit him following a monthly sorority meeting. It was Saturday February 1,1997, Black History Month; and the Case of the Century Part 11 was the focus of our curious interest.

I had brought from the meeting a love kit with a Valentine message that contained a daily prayer, a rubber band, band-aid, paper clip, toothpick, candy, string and a penny, seemingly to help us cope with the verdict. Laughing, I read to him a typed statement from the kit that explained the purpose of each item: "'Daily prayer-for our busy days. Rubber Band: a reminder to be flexible. Band-aid -for healing. Paper clip: for holding together. Toothpick: reminder not to be picky. Candy: to remind you that God is with you through the bitter and sweet times. String: to help tie up loose ends. Penny: to share God's wealth; to have enough 'cents to realize what a valuable person you are.'"

My husband laughed heartily, then asked that I read the Love Kit's prayer.

Tearfully, I read the timely prayer my sorority sisters had fashioned, it seemed, just for me: "'Dear Lord, thank you for your constant Love which continues even when we may not sense it and when we feel depressed.'"

"Perfect," John shouted. "Write that down, Alice."

"We are writing addicts," I said, kissing his forehead.

To be truthful, we were writing as a narcotic to numb the pain. But, writer's block was threatening to intrude, and I found all thoughts focused on the The Trial of the Century as though something forceful was compelling me to stay tuned because there was a universal message blowing in the wind.

Earlier my husband had said of the June 12, 1994 deaths that the tragedy of life isn't death but it's what we let die within us. And now he said that Patty, like all spirits who love, had held on to love and dwelled among us in the kingdom of heaven.

"After all, her life was trying to tell us that we're all children of *Genesis*," he calmly added.

"*Genesis's* children?" I repeated, frightened that he was again in solitude with his deeper self, moving further into brighter lights and ready to steal away, too. The last thing I needed at this time was another loved one's flight into eternity. After all, we both had been pensively watching the Simpson Case and had watched Bill Moyers' *Genesis: A Living Conversation* series on WPBT-Channel 2. The conversation was exploding in our minds like an atom (Adam) bomb. Father Dionne had taught me about *Genesis*.

"Has the Simpson case sent us back into that prehistorical subject again to express our psychological thoughts and feelings versus *Genesis*' doctrine of original sin?" I had asked, adjusting his pillow, then kissing his glossy, golden nose. Even with his disability, he still looked distinguished and courageous.

"Keep writing; you'll discover it," he whispered, further implying that we humans can achieve self realization by self reference. He counseled that solitude is an institution of learning within oneself and a basic human need that is often neglected.

"You're so right," I said, remembering that ever since the beginning of the case, he declared that watching it on television was a form of solitude. When I mentioned this, he recalled the statement and smiled his "Oh boy!"

"And silence is one of the most impressive events of our life, even as we watch the Case on TV," he added.

"But, it wasn't televised this time, therefore we didn't have the luxury of watching it in its entirety; we could only watch excerpts," I said dismally, adjusting his bed covers and re-reminding him of Edward Gibbon's statement that solitude is the school of genius,..and especially of poets, novelists, composers, painters, sculptors who spent their time alone. "He and other writers wondered how those who don't write, compose or paint escape the madness, the melancholia, the panic fear which is inherent in the human situation... especially the madness of this case!"

"But, Alice, don't they know.. that...life's..a..series.. of problem.. solving.. situations?" he asked, then began talking about the power of solitude in human life.

I told him that there was something about solitude and the creative personality that I needed to research because many writers were prone to depression. Some of them, like Anne Sexton, committed suicide by sticking her head in a lighted gas oven. Perhaps her creative powers were beginning to be paralyzed by depression. I didn't tell him that worrying about his MS had often left me paralyzed by depression and that's why I became addicted to writing about the wisdom of love. And now here comes this Trial of the Century and it seemed I'd put my world on hold.

Pausing into John's stretched, grayish-brown eyes, I added: "Solitude is excellent and I understand that writers do their best writing in solitude and can become obsessed with it. But one needs interpersonal relationships. We must love one another or die!"

"Solitude..helps...you.. to..feel.. love, Alice," he remonstrated, looking at *The Miami Herald* newspaper I had brought to share with him.

I nodded my agreement. "And heaven knows, sweetheart, your illness has provided you with long periods of solitude which we've wisely used and which has become the basis of our literary world. And because of this input, our writings have earned us many awards, thanks to passion, pain and suffering."

"And solitude," he added and smiled, then repeated that even watching television is a form of solitude when you're locked into the story and interpreting what you see by using your own wisdom, not someone else's.

I smiled, too, Why? Because listening to others interpret the case was oftentimes disturbing to me...especially in my aloneness and recurring states of loneliness. But, I needed to continue discovering the spiritual world within, and whatever comments were made about the case would not upset me.

"It is educational, sweetheart," I said. "Sally had told me in the beginning of the case that as long as I believe that some of the evidence against Simpson was probably planted, I'll always believe that he probably isn't guilty."

"Alice, that's why we have a jury."

"But this civil jury is all White, John."

"Perhaps that doesn't matter, Alice. The jury in the criminal trial was mostly Black." He adjusted his eyeglasses and stared at me. "You've gotta have faith in the legal system."

Like hell, I thought to myself, recalling all the injustices we Blacks have experienced. After all, he and I were in the group of peaceful demonstrators that got locked up during the Civil Rights Movement back in 1957. Had he forgotten?

My thoughts were interrupted by John's " *Try to keep an open mind and please take care of your health*" litany.

"My health?" I replied, jumping up from the chair and pacing the floor, perplexed. "Do you have reference to my mental health?"

"Mental and physical."

"Oh." I knew he had reference to the mammogram appointments I kept canceling because I wanted to watch the case. Cancer, like MS, is such a mean disease. Perhaps we humans need to bring a case against Mother Nature for child abuse. The case could be called *The People vs Mother Nature*.

My husband and I talked about my state of denial of being an at-risk victim and the urgent need to write about it. He felt I needed to continue to write all areas of frustrations and stress factors out of my system including domestic abuse.

He was right, because by doing this, I had learned from past experiences, that writing would ward-off-depressions and save my own life from whatever was troubling me. Perhaps this was my mission...to write the thoughts and feelings stemming from the writing block!

"My Mission!" I shouted, both fists raised in midair. It seemed my whole universe lit up and I did the Electric Slide across the room to the melody of John's sweet sounding laughter. But, I was completely unaware that it would be a painful mission...almost akin to Anne Sexton's had I not fought to become impregnably in love with the universe. My obsession with the Case of the Century was driving me insane.

Later that evening when I returned home, I went for a two-mile walk then returned and continued working on the manuscript far into the night. Meditatively typing, I continued putting the meaning of Patty's humble life and lives of other humble victims, to words because they brought a unique, age-old spiritual message that was challenging us to stop the violence and love one another; and to let our love for one another be expressed through deeds of concern and through deeds of kindness and mercy. Unfortunately and oftentimes, we are too busy with our own individual agendas or in our own selfish worlds to see the message and the messenger that comes in all races, colors and nationalities.

The book of *Genesis* kept flashing before me, revealing that ever since the beginning of time, we've been sent spirits to show us through example, the way to feel love for each other...the way to express love that leads to the kingdom of heaven which is within us. But, our egos tend to dominate our existence.

Again, the book of *Genesis*_surfaced when the word "ego" slipped into the context. I thought about John's implication that *Genesis* is our lineage in that, on the positive side, our moral sentiments do have an innate basis.

Patty's philosophy, "Love Finds Expression through Kindness and Concern," is a basic truth in *Genesis* that has mellowed with the ages, and one which John and I had learned, from his illness, to embrace. As a patient and caregiver, life had taught us that love is the ultimate virtue toward which all other qualities point... such as joy, peace, gentleness, goodness, faith, meekness, longsuffering and temperance.

The book of *Genesis* had told the story ages ago and now, in solitude, I felt that we offsprings of *Genesis* needed to reflect on it.

Unknowingly, and while awaiting the verdict of the civil trial, I was beginning to become more obsessed with solitude.

4

"What is necessary after all, is only this: solitude, vast inner solitude. To walk inside yourself and meet no one for hours. That is what you must be able to attain."
- Rainer Maria Rilke

Feeling sleepless and in the solitude of thought, my mind pondered over love's wisdom as anxious fingers continued to dance across computer keys recording yesteryear's thoughts Thoughts that were cluttering my mind ...creating writer's block and inflicting pain and suffering, paralyzing creativeness.

Someone had said that when we accept our pain and suffering as a guard, prodding us into undertaking the solitary, difficult, painful and often unrewarding work of exploring our own depths and recording what we find, we can escape being overwhelmed by them. Perhaps so, but this Trial of the Century drama was trying to make that impossible.

Again, I asked the universe: "Aren't we here to find our self-realization through the service of others? Haven't we been repeatedly taught that the shortest way to the Creator is to bring comfort to the soul of our neighbor?"

I thought about *Genesis*; but this time, I thought about its meaning...the book that conveyed betrayal, sibling rivalry, jealousy, wanting to strike out at one's neighbor, and all "the thousand pangs that flesh is heir to."

Aware of the similarities to modern society, I continued my silent questioning about the book of *Genesis* which started with the creation of the world, then hurried on toward Adam and Eve's temptation and fall, the murder of Abel by his brother Cain in which the ego which is capable of viciousness at worst, projected our inherited selfishness; and the story of Noah. Then, there were Abraham and Sarah's fertility problems and the attendant strife this caused. There was Sodom and Gomorrah. And at the end, there was Joseph's abandonment by his brothers and then the forgiveness that healed family wounds exemplifying that love finds expression through kindness and concern.

Now frustrated and frightened, I said to the universe, "It seems all modern society is learning the art of living from the book of *Genesis*! I find that even my own creative writing is drawn to its format. You need to help us understand *Genesis* and do some stocktaking. But I can see that you're already helping us by sending The Simpson University and to help us along, you 've sent Bill Moyers and his *Genesis: A Living Conversation*" whose writings have been exploding within our consciousness like an atom bomb since these trials.

But something inside me was yearning for an authentic experience. Something inside me was searching for an in-depth meaning on the art of being human within oneself. I thought about the Simpson trials and Mark Fuhrman's taped conversation, then pulled a research folder from the lateral files that spoke to the subject of racism. Pensively, I re-read *The Miami Herald* newspaper clippings implicating man's inhumanity to man. The clippings spoke of the free forum, "*Hate in America*," that had been scheduled at the University of Miami Law School October, 1996, perhaps due to Fuhrman's testimony.

Before the civil trial began, I had read an article announcing the forum in *The Miami Herald*. Recalling this, I rushed back into the office files and retrieved the stack of newspaper clippings, thumbing furiously through them to locate the write-up. Finding it, I read with serious concern, admitting that the universe profits from our madness just as much as it profits from our sanity.

The bombings of African-American churches. Racial, ethnic and religious prejudices on the Internet. Hate speech on university campuses.

The latest trends in prejudice in the United States and other topics will be discussed at a free forum, "Hate in America," at 7 p.m. Wednesday at the University of Miami Law School, 1311 Miller Dr., Coral Gables.

Hate and bigotry in all their forms still represent a major challenge to American society," said Arthur Teitelbaum of the Anti-Defamation League, and organizer of the event. "They are a poison in the bloodstream of America."

The law school's Center for Ethics and Public-Service and the Urban League of Greater Miami are the other sponsors of the forum, which will feature a keynote speech by Herald Publisher David Lawrence, Jr....

..."Miami is where much of the rest of the country will be in 20 years," Teitelbaum said. "We are intensely multicultural and passing through constant demographic change and experiencing stress in interpersonal relations as a result."

"Multicultural!" I repeated. "My school of thought!"

Clipping the announcement from the half-page, my scissors cutting through a headline that read "Miami man is chased, fatally shot," I paused and painfully skimmed the story which told of policemen investigating the death of a 27-year old man who was chased down the street by someone and slain.

Then, ironically, the "Of Note" headline beneath it read: Red Cross honors woman's life-saving CPR. I paused and quickly skimmed the 6-line paragraph: *Annabella Fenyo of Miami Beach received a Certificate of Merit last week from the American Red Cross of Greater Miami & The Keys for saving the life of her father, John Fenyo, by using cardiopulmonary resuscitation. Annabella Fenyo had taken a Red Cross CPR course four days before her father's heart attack.*

"Miracles of the universe, intuitions, domestic nonviolence," I said, my mind recalling the abused wife, Anabelle, in my unfinished novel, *Kennetta*. Thanking the universe and *The Miami*

Herald for sharing with us an example, just as *Genesis* did, that love, indeed, finds expression through kindness and concern, I now wanted to also focus on domestic nonviolence.

Questioning my unending thoughts and feelings, I realized that the capacity to be alone seemed a valuable resource. "It's the kind of resource that facilitates learning, thinking innovation, examining human behavior and its roots, and examining the inner conflicts of oneself," I boasted to the computer, unaware that I was becoming too preoccupied with the habit even though I had used it to counteract my Anorexia Nervosa and Bulemia, I was creating another outlet that could be even more detrimental. Well, at least I wasn't starving to death or eating up my frustrations while the jury was deliberating over the weekend.

"Being alone can also serve as a healing function for our mental and physical health, especially those of us who're becoming writing addicts as a cop-out to avoid other responsibilities like waiting for a verdict from a predominately White jury that can drive one crazy because the verdict might send us a most disturbing message that justice is in the race of the beholder. Even while I was locked in solitude and telling my mind to forget the case, I seemed unable to feel the contentment it should have been bringing. Perhaps I was thinking too seriously and experimenting with the uses we make of solitude in times of bereavement, or depression, or in escaping from the stressful pressures of daily life, or in communicating with the universe, and in expressing our deepest self.

But, even so, my thoughts and feelings still had a constant and passionate longing to break free from life's sorrows. On the other hand, I needed to find a happy medium and deal with the issue that depression is part of the experience of every human being. My analyst had said that depression varies in depth and severity, but not in its essential nature; and that no one has a monopoly on problems.

I told him that I thought I had a monopoly on problems until

I learned to stop trying to control other people's lives and take care of my own. When he asked how did I arrive at such wisdom, I quoted a response from Gandhi when someone praised him for his compassionate politics: "I am here to serve no one else but myself, to find my own self-realization through the service to others."

Suddenly, I began thinking again about the civil trial and wondering why was O.J. being tried again when he had already been acquitted by a jury of his peers. Perhaps the universe was speaking because he had abused his wife whom he had sworn to love, honor and protect. Maybe he forgot to let his attitude be gratitude...gratitude for a beautiful wife, children, money and fame. Or, maybe he forgot that Nature never forgives.

I told the universe that lots of men beat their wives and that I didn't believe that O.J. had time to commit those murders in that short length of time. Although he, in a fit of anger, could have done it just as John almost blew my brains out. Even when I wrote *Mysterious Stranger Aboard*, my parents were shocked to learn that John was abusive because to them, he was always such a gentleman.. And I had the nerve to fire back at them with vengeance for calling my John an abusive husband.

In all seriousness, I even wanted to verbally attack our African American family physician, Dr. John McAdory, for telling my African American lawyer, Atty. Leon Sharp, that my husband was sometimes very abusive toward me and seemed to be an angry man but that it probably was due to his illness. When did our family doctor tell my lawyer this? It happened when John became totally disabled to the point that he would be needing a legal guardian and our doctors and minister suggested I begin the precedings while John was able to successfully respond to court assigned doctors designated to make this decision. Otherwise, I would encounter unsurmountable legal problems trying to protect John and my investments. Dr. McAdory had to respond to the court assigned doctors' medical forms. The negotiated report revealed this abusive behavior, not to harm John's reputation, but to let the court know the truth. At first, I could not believe that our kind family doctor would say this ugly thing about my sweet John, then I recalled the many times I had rushed to the doctor's busy office in tears, telling him about John threatening me and running me out of the house with his walking cane in his fits of anger. Sometimes I was afraid that he would awaken at night and, due to post war syndrome, clobber me with that walking cane while I was asleep. I also told the doctor that my husband was not taking the ten milligrams of Millaril, a mood depressant, he had prescribed. Because John had high respect for our family doctor, we were able to stay on top of the problems and survive the physical tragedies that await many of us abused wives if both man and wife don't seek professional help.

Why did I stay and fight for our marriage? Because I love my husband. If I did not love him, I would've gotten the hell out of the marriage. He wasn't always abusive. He was sick and needed help. Lots of kind, loving husbands are sick... physically and mentally.. and need professional help.

Tears clouded my eyes and I continued with a prayer: Nicole, please help us women, your abused sisters of all races and nationalities, to wake up and fight against this evil behavior that destroys happy marriages and families. Please don't let these trials be a gauge of race relations; rather, let them advance us all forward as a world of united people. With this, your life, Nicole, will be a monument to womanhood. Tell Ron to help the men stop the violence while you help us women become more responsible mothers inasmuch as we women, like the biblical character Eve, are the ones who give birth to the seed that's planted within us. Let both your spirits guide us to move beyond the racial barriers that are blocking vision, and guide us to build for eternity, In so doing, your lives will be a Monument To Human Brotherhood.

Suddenly, and in the stillness, lines from the inspirational hymn, *Where Cross the Crowded Ways of Life* by Frank Mason North and William Gardiner eased into my thoughts. It is a song that I had learned while attending Atlanta University (now known as Clark-Atlanta University) and while I was trying to survive an abusive marriage. I began singing it silently, tears flooding my eyes:

"Where cross the crowded ways of life,
Where sound the cries of race and clan;
Above the noise of selfish strife
We hear thy voice, O Son of Man.

"In haunts of wretchedness and need
In shadowed thresholds dark with fears
From paths where hide the lures of greed
We catch the vision of Thy tears."

After singing the four verses, I dried my eyes, grateful that I had formed the habit of memorizing songs that were dear to my heart because they were like personal prayers of hope. Adding to this feeling of hope, Shurtleff and Smart inspirational hymn, *Lead On, O King Eternal*, surfaced to add more meaning to the message.

"Lead on, O King Eternal, 'till sins fierce war shall cease,
And holiness shall whisper the sweet amen of peace;
For not with swords loud clashing nor roll or stirring drums,
But deeds of love and mercy the heavenly kingdom comes."

I still wanted to break free from life's sorrows and disturbing thoughts about the racial divide through understanding, and find a happy balance between my inner and outer world so that bouts of depression would not interfere with my creative endeavor, unless it is true that depressive temperament is particularly common among writers. I also needed to enter into a consultation with the universe to find out whether or not this was predetermined, and how does *Genesis* fit into the various personality patterns?

The universe has a unique way of responding to our innermost questions. My mind was immediately drawn to the Pastoral Letter on Racism written by Archbishop Edward A. McCarthy who was, at the time of the book of letters, Archbishop of Miami. Fortunately, I was a member of the Archdiocesan Black Pastoral Council which he chaired following the 1980 racial riot.

The racial riot was fueled by a myriad of racial injustices and had made Blacks feel like a lighted "fuse" in "confused." When love is not expressed through kindness and concern, life can be confusing. In our book, *Mysterious Stranger Aboard*, John and I had written about the riot, and some of the injustices which my protagonist was ticking off on his fingers as he continued his recountal were as follows:

...A Black teenage boy was shot by an off-duty White policeman during a struggle which, by the officer's later admission, never took place. No indictment .

...A Black school teacher and his son were beaten by White policemen in their own home on a "mistaken" cocaine raid. No indictment!

...A Black commissioner was suspended for allegedly operating illegal bingo!

...A Black superintendent of schools...one of the finest educators in the nation...was tried by an All White jury for a crime which, the White accuser later admitted, was filled with untruths!

...Black Haitians were turned away as unwelcome refugees while fair-skinned Hispanics were welcome.

...An 11-year old Black girl was sexually molested by a White patrolman who received no probation.

...An all White jury acquitted three White policemen for the motorcycle killing of Marine Veteran Arthur McDuffie.

The Black community and ninety percent of the White community were appalled at the decision of the "not Guilty" verdict by the all White jury in the McDuffie case. Enraged, young Black men exploded in anger and a racial riot ensued. The disturbance lasted three days. John and I wrote the conclusion: "*Miami survived as firemen, policemen and concerned citizens quenched the last embers of blazes that had reduced scores of businesses to charred shells as street crews hosed off the blood of fourteen people beaten or shot to death, and 3,800 National Guardsmen withdrew from patrolling a forty-block by sixty-block area of the shaken 'Magic City' we loved so dearly.*"

Following the riot, I was asked to serve on the Pastoral Council on Inter-Racial Relations. As our leader, Archbishop McCarthy expressed serious concern about the problems of hate and social evils that were at the root of racial disturbances. He and his staff worked endlessly with other community leaders of all nationalities to help permeate and strengthen the democratic system of justice. Then in 1983, he published the letter on inter-racial relations in the light of the gospel. He expressed his gratitude for the assistance of the Black Pastoral Council and the Archdiocesan Office of Catholic Community Services.

Under the title "*One People Under God*," the soul-searching letter spoke firmly on sensitive issues under the following sub-titles: *How Christlike Are Community Relations in South Florida? Why Racial Minorities Are Aggrieved; How does the Racial Reality Challenge Our Faith? How Should Catholics Respond to Racism? A Call To Action, Our Families and Our Neighborhood; Our Archdiocese, Our Community; Education; Economic Development; Employment; Juvenile Justice*; and *The Administration of Justice*. In the concluding statement of the letter, I excerpted the following from the Archbishop's text:

What is to be our personal response to racism? First of all, we must examine our own attitudes and behavior. We must become aware of latent prejudices we have. We must criticize our vocabulary in order to eliminate inherited words or phrases that continue to reflect a judgment of inferiority. We must expressly reject racial stereotypes, slurs and jokes. We will never know the hurt that has been caused by "innocent" fun. We must become more sensitive to and knowledgeable of the authentic human values and cultural contributions of each racial group in our community. Finally, we must become more aware of how the structures in our society work and what are the people implication of business and political policies that are being enacted. We must be aware of the systemic causes of our problems and not just the individual expressions of them.

Racism is a radical evil which cannot be conquered by human effort alone. We need the strength of the Lord Jesus and the healing power of His Spirit in the multi-racial, multi-cultural situation which is ours here in South Florida. ...We need each other. We need each other's differences to reflect the multi-faceted beauty of the people of God.

.....Whatever we do, our efforts need to be strengthened by our fervent prayers.

"Christian love," as the Vatican Council reminds us, "truly extends to all without distinction of race, social condition or religion. It looks for neither gain nor gratitude. For as God has loved us with a spontaneous love, so also the faithful should in their charity care for the human person himself."

After typing the powerfully-phrased excerpt, my mind was locked into its contents and the many other subjects of deep interest and concern that were included in the book of Pastoral Letters. I was moved to tears of joy! The Archbishop stated that as a community of love, we are a people committed to all the virtues, all the forms of goodness! "We need to be builders of unity in our families, our neighborhoods, our communities, our nation and our world."

In one of the council meetings, the Archbishop implied that bigotry is a tree of many branches. "It involves Whites against Blacks, Blacks against Whites, Latins against non-Hispanics. It cuts across grains of religions and point of view. Bigotry is an insidious, invisible poison that can permeate a city block, or a whole town. Much of it seems to spring from our own protective instincts to preserve" our identities, our territories, and our customs.

Genesis! my thoughts exploded and my mind flipped through the pages of biblical history to pinpoint instinctive patterns of human behavior. It has been said that conversation enriches understanding, but solitude is the school of knowledge.

With deeds of love and mercy the heavenly kingdom comes.

5

A human being is part of the whole that we call the universe, a part limited in time and space. He experiences himself, his thoughts and feelings that should embrace all of nature. (Albert Einstein)

"We cannot bring harm to others when we retreat to solitude and see ourselves in them," I said to myself the following morning, staring at the computer and wondering why was I up again at two o'clock. Did I want to write about Patty or did I unconsciously want to hear more news about the civil trial, or maybe bake some brownies for the bag lady and me? I wondered where was the bag lady and what was her name? Could it be Hester?

"According to Eastern religion, only in constant meditation can the experience of seeing ourselves in others be attained."

Feeling somewhat uncomfortable about talking aloud to myself and sounding like a loonie, I began speaking silently into my computer and all nature, including metaphysics.

But this was solitude! And I felt helpless being drawn deeper into it with an unusual sense of pleasure, and running away from the fear of pain...the fear of a verdict that would send us a disturbing message that even with the teachings of great leaders, we're still into *Genesis*.

Even so, when we retreat to solitude, the experience of breaking free from life's sorrows can be attained without retreating into fantasy as, it has been said, many writers of fiction often do.

Pausing, I wondered about *Genesis* and fiction writing. We

writers had been told to tell the truth but tell it with a slant. I now wondered did our creative writing teachers learn this method of storytelling from *Genesis*... and even, perhaps other books of the Bible.

The universe said "yes" and that some of the episodes are parables that presuppose *Genesis* account of creation and of the Fall, and relates the covenant-keeping character of the Creator as told by the prophets.

"Good! Inasmuch as you're beginning to answer me, I'm gonna keep pressing on," I said aloud, then recalled that it is in quietness and in solitude that we hear His voice.

But my mind wouldn't stop singing the inspirational hymn, *Higher Ground*, by Johnson Oatman and Charles Gabriel, or was this the universe singing it for me, just as it did *Psalm 91* when I heard my heart singing the verse "*My heart has no desire to stay where doubts arise and fears dismay.*"

I'm pressing on the upward way, new heights I'm gaining every day...

Certainly the Simpson trials were taking me to new heights. I felt as though I was gaining new heights every day listening to the news media, even if the media was brainwashing me as Sally had said the week before she died. I now wondered did the disturbing message of the trials contribute to her sudden death.

But breaking free from life's sorrows and writing non-fiction meant I needed to continuously cultivate understandings by conversing with my higher consciousness to experience problems not as sorrow, but more as a joy. After all, Jesus came to spread joy...to teach us the joy of loving one another. His teachings led us to believe that whatever happens in a lifetime has been planned and decreed from all eternity by a God of love because of love. I wondered about The Trial of the Century and felt that I was becoming paranoid. Strange as it may seem, I felt like joining the bag lady.

According to *The Miami Herald*, Dr. Ruth Richards, in her

book entitled *Creativity and the Healthy Mind*, said that: "People who have experienced emotional extremes, who have been forced to confront a huge range of feelings and who have successfully coped with those adversities, could end up with a richer organization in memory, a richer palette to work with." In like manner, I recalled another author implying that: although creativity is obviously an essential element in many professions, the link between creativity and mental instability is more pronounced in the arts than in other fields.

Well, thanks to you Mother Nature. Is that why the jails are filled with talented artists whose gifts have been stifled because they didn't understand your little peek-a-boo games?

While it is true that the solution of the problems I was seeing is to live in a way that would make them opportunities for further growth, I needed to write deeper, plowing into the roots of my thoughts and feelings to root out the causes of depression so that I can feel free to write. My analyst once said that a cure that destroys the depression might destroy the intensity of my creative skills. Being ungrateful and depressed, I've never acknowledged that I had creative skills. My "never" was beginning to sound like O.J. Simpson's. He was accused of using the n-word, except it wasn't the one Fuhrman used; it was the word "Never."

And now I was feeling depressed.

"One of the reasons why you're depressed is probably because of your ingratitude," the analyst had counseled. I felt like hating him for speaking the truth. I was grateful for the civil trial, but I wanted to see it on live TV so that I could help form my own opinions.

On second thought, and perhaps it was the universe speaking to me, I wondered whether or not ridding myself totally of depression would be detrimental to my writing skills, inasmuch as most of my intense writing is done during periods of depression. My analyst told me to write whatever I was feeling, and whatever I was searching for would slowly surface. I found this to be true when John and I were writing *Mysterious Stranger Aboard.* The book unfolded, and I was astounded! Afterwards, John and I realized that 'creative apperception' is what makes us humans feel that life is worth living. In creating our life story, we were able to restore a lost unity within our inner world as well as produce a story which had a real existence in the external world.

Still engaged in meditative writing, my mind suggested that I enter into conversation with the universe which had become my constant companion and therapist. By living the questions now, I believed that I would someday, while completing this book, live my way into the answer. Besides, I wanted to focus on Patty's philosophy...and maybe it was her suggestion. We know so little about the spiritual world.

Thinking of the bag lady and wondering was she named Hester, I eased into the white leather recliner and sat tall; eyes closed. Then pausing for five minutes of silent meditation, I entered into an exercise of deep muscle relaxation. Later, and still in a relaxed state, I asked:

"If love is expressed through such simplistic actions as kindness and concern, and if man is a social being who needs the companionship of other human beings from cradle to grave, then why did you let this thing happen to the Simpsons? Why is it so difficult for man to understand how to love one another which is the gateway to the kingdom of heaven within himself?" my mind asked into the stillness of lavender morning.

"Aren't we all searching for peace of mind..contentment?

"Why isn't there a story in *Genesis* that emphasizes this? Why did Noah get drunk following the flood when he arrived at his destination with his ark filled with chosen survivors? Did he feel compassion for those victims who were drowning in that flood...especially the little children? If so, is this why he got drunk?

"Why do some humans (perhaps in the footsteps of Noah) still celebrate accomplishments with strong drinks (strong drinks that trigger domestic violence, drunk driving and other sorrows that create pain and suffering like that darn apple...and I bet it wasn't even good)? Why did Simpson celebrate with drinks when he won the criminal trial? Was he following Noah's pattern of behavior?

"Isn't accomplishing the goal a high enough high when we give our Creator the glory? Why are many of your talented writers prone to depression, heavy drinking, heavy smoking, suicide? Is it because most of them dismiss religion as superstition? Our visiting priest jokingly said that 'every time you see four priests dining you wonder where is the fifth.' Even so, I've been told that practically all writers express strong belief in the Creator just as Noah and all priests and religious leaders. Our visiting priest also won an award at our 1996 Women's Guild Annual Christmas Brunch when he dramatically sung the song: "Come To Me My Alcoholic Baby" with lines so humorous, we cracked our sides with laughter. Lord, it feels good to laugh together in a spiritual setting.

"Frankly, I don't believe in organized religion, but I have a firm belief in our Creator, and that we all are the Creator's children regardless of what religion. No religion has a monopoly on the Creator.

"When I think of our Creator, I'm overly overwhelmed! Absolutely speechless! And when I meditate, the split second of His brilliance blinds me! Words cannot express the feeling. But the *Psalms* , and the inspirational hymns that sing praises paint an excellent picture of my thoughts and feelings. Thank you for the gifted writers of the Holy Bible, and the book of *Psalms*, and inspirational hymns and religious ministers who know the Creator and share their talents with us!

"The *Reader's Digest Bible* said that *Song of Solomon* isn't about the church as the synopsis in the Holy Bible said. *Reader's Digest* said *Song of Solomon* contains no outright mention of religion, and the word God does not occur even once. The book is more like love poetry. It's a dialogue between a Jewish maiden and her lover, with several other people present as onlookers. Am I correct in seeing this as an example of love being expressed through kindness and concern? I'm searching.

"By the way, why did King Solomon need so many wives (didn't he have about 80) inasmuch as he was filled with the spirit of God as written?

"Anyway, let's get back to our good buddies in *Genesis* who started all this commotion. Shouldn't Adam's name be Atom inasmuch as his will (so-called free will) created an atomic bomb that is still exploding in today's society?"

Then pausing, I thought about the thesis from *Genesis* that preoccupy modern society.. I thought about the unending search for self and the continuous search for innerpeace, universal peace social justice and brotherly love. I though about the *Genesis* society of murder, rape, incest, adultery, child-rearing problems, greed, rage, jealousy, family feuds, environmental desecration like our Florida Everglades, caregiving like Joseph gave his family. I then wondered about the other suffering families that were victims of the famine.

Even caregiving can be selfish, I thought to myself. O. J. wasn't selfish because he helped many families and people of all nationalities. And now the system wants all his money. Are we missing a spiritual lesson here? Nobody likes poverty; it's a curse. But, the greatest curse is the absence of unconditional love. Check that out.

Examining this point of interest, I recalled how over-protective I am of my family and of John in seeing that his medical needs are taken care of; and how protective I've become of other patients following my enlightenment. I thought about the difficult time I sometimes have in learning to see myself in others, then asked the universe:

"Like our ancestors in *Genesis*, are we designed by natural selection (close kin selection or 'you help me and I'll help you (reciprocal altruism)' selection) to conceal selfish motives from ourselves as evolutionary psychologists believe? Isn't it true that beneath this kind of familial love is malice toward our relatives' rivals and that's why we engage in bloody wars, feeling we're right and our rival's wrong? Even our religious faiths are prejudiced toward each other. Why? How does this fit into the Simpson trials regarding racism? Please help us to understand so that we might continue to grow more spiritually.

"After *Genesis* years, why are we so slow in making moral progress, and is this the Creator's will? If so, please help us to understand so that we can follow His divine leadership instead of lingering in confusion. In my world, confusion breeds depression. Is this a part of spiritual growth?

"According to some of your prophets, we act only from God's will, and that the more we do, the more perfect our actions are and the more we have peace of mind. I do experience this beautiful peace of mind when I believe that the Creator is guiding my every actions. Is the Creator guiding the actions of Simpson's trial lawyers? Johnny Cochran, Jr? Robert Shapiro? F. Lee Bailey? Barry Scheck and the other professionals? What about prosecutors Christopher Darden who has a part of Christ's name, and Marcia Clark who made us women proud of her performance, and other members of their professional team? If you were guiding these actions, the whole thought stops conversation. Even in the civil trial we will say... 'let Thy will be done.'

"Is free will a blessing and a curse? Do we actually have free will? If we actually have free will, then it is true that intuition (direct perception of truth) is the highest endeavor and the highest virtue of the mind. Please help me to always follow my intuition inasmuch as I believe that it is you revealing your truth to me. About that mammogram...do I actually have free will or am I biting into that forbidden apple (not the 'bitten' apple on my Macintosh LC 11 computer)?

"Truly, there are people who lack love, or who do no feel the presence of love within, but are they considered tools in the hands of the Creator who serve unconsciously and are destroyed in the service? Is this their choice because of a lack of understanding? Isn't this why the crucified Jesus asked the Creator to forgive those who crucified him? Was this the Roman soldiers' choice? Is The Trial of the Century related to any of these experiences?

"It is my understanding that all things that the Creator revealed to the prophets as being necessary for salvation are written by them in the form of laws. In view of this understanding, the prophets invented a whole parable that's given in *Genesis*. First, the Creator had revealed the means of salvation and destruction, (reward and punishment) and was the cause of them all. The prophets described the creator as a king and lawgiver.

"Spinoza believes that the prophets arranged all their words more according to the parable than according to the truth, and that we should follow virtue not in obedience to law, but from love because it is the most excellent of all things. He believes that the prohibition given to Adam consisted solely in this: the Creator revealed to Adam that eating of the tree caused death, just as He reveals to us, through our natural intellect, that poison (hatefulness, greed, lust, envy, jealousy, and all the anti-social behavior we see in *Genesis* and carried over into present-day society, etc.) is deadly. The Creator did this to make Adam more perfect in knowledge. (Eastern philosophers believe that: "He who increases his knowledge, increases his sorrow." Did the bag lady increase her knowledge?).

"With this understanding, I am led to believe that Adam did not sin when he ate the forbidden fruit; he was testing the hypothesis in his decision, or determined will, to eat the forbidden fruit. Well, somebody had to test it for validity and set an example for us just as Jesus of Nazareth had to test the validity of love to set an example for us who are still eating the forbidden fruit we inherited from *Genesis* as stated in the parable written by prophets.

"According to the story, the Creator did not tell Adam that the kingdom of heaven is within him because according to the parable, Adam was already within the kingdom of heaven. Luckily he wasn't thrown out for biting into the apple (inasmuch as the prophets constantly..and in my belief erroneously, described the Creator as a man, now angry, now merciful, now gripped by jealousy and suspicion, and even deceived by the devil. It is my belief that the Creator is divine love. (Mother Nature has taught us children this, but when we consider the Simpson drama, we sometimes feel that she can be an evil little witch. Why did you let hate come in and destroy that beautiful relationship that was loved by both White and Black?).

"Adam became wiser; and according to life teachings, a wise man is hardly ever troubled in spirit, but being conscious of himself, of his Creator of his neighbor and of spiritual things, possesses true serenity of mind. Why isn't Adam considered a hero instead of a curse inasmuch as he was used as a controlled subject (i.e.guinea pig)? Don't we humans love the wisdom of knowing what is right and wrong? Wasn't his experience another form of crucifixion? Why didn't the voice tell him that 'no good deed goes unpunished?'

"When Adam ate the forbidden fruit of the tree of knowledge, Mother Nature should have told him that, and I repeat, 'he that increases his knowledge increases his sorrows.' That's why it's said that to enter the kingdom of heaven, we must become like little children who see nothing but love. Their trust is in love! Love, not thought (knowledge) is the greatest creation of life. Mother Nature has taught us that the universe spins on the energy of love! Our experiences have shown us that the Creator is love; even if He did send us Miamians Hurricane Andrew that scared hell out of us children. We should have sued Mother Nature for child abuse; but she taught us to forgive. Anyway, your prophets tell us that we are not only created out of love but exist out of love.

"When the prophets named our first human beings Adam and Eve, was this a euphemism for atom and evil?. We see synonymous meanings here. Was the atom bomb we dropped on Hiroshima and Nagasaki, Japan evil? Or, was this the will of the Creator?

"My reason for longing to know the answers to the myriad of

questions is because life has taught us that the more we understand particular things, the more we understand and love our Creator, ourselves and our neighbor. Loving the Creator is our greatest happiness because His love for us is expressed through kindness and concern. Are these trials, Simpson I & Simpson 11, going to divide us? Do you have to destroy to rebuild like you did with Noah and the Ark or better still... when you sent your angry Hurricane Andrew? Guess what? We love the new South Dade. We enjoyed helping one another. Thanks for the opportunity to love and help each other. Now, please let these trials show us how to move higher in spiritual love.

"Let's be realistic, every being in the world longs to be always happy, without any experiences of sorrow. Remember the popular song "*Don't Worry, Be Happy*" by Bobby McFarren and how it became a number one hit overnight as soon as it hit Blockbuster Video & Records! Even former President Bush quoted the calming title during his administration when the economy was making us noble Americans worried about our nation's future. My husband tactfully added his comment when he smiled and said 'Don't worry be happy 'cause nothing's gonna be all right anyhow ...unless we learn to take things as they are and not as we want them to be.' Mother Nature has taught me that as long as we try to force everything to go according to the way we think it ought to, we're gonna always be unhappy.

"At the same time, everyone loves himself best. My analyst, in his counseling efforts to help me learn to love myself , would often say: ' to you, YOU are the most important person in the world.' I had a difficult time perceiving this truth. Suddenly I realized that if I felt this way about myself, and I learned to treat my neighbor as I would have him treat me, I would treat him as though he were, to himself, the most important person in the world. This perception would enable me to respect his right to feel this way.

"Love is caused by joy,... as in the case of the biblical character

Joseph when he remonstrated the forgiveness that heals family wounds. Therefore, joy must be inside oneself. In order to realize this inherited joy, somewhat like the kind that we experience when we're asleep, it's very important for one to know oneself. And the best way to really know oneself is in solitude where the mind can be opened to the value of spiritual transformation in everyday experiences.

"Solitude is a powerful gift that enables us to look deeply into our thoughts and feelings to achieve self realization by self reference to the spiritual world, especially when we feel that there is something elusive and missing from our lives.

"For this reason, we continue longing to find the Kingdom of Heaven within ourselves so that we can see our fortunes and misfortunes as spiritual gifts, find ourselves, and rise to our highest potentials...which is, as Deepak Chopra has said, boundless!. But, universe, you need to do something because I feel like I'm working hard and getting absolutely nowhere."

Slowly, a voice whispered, *Let your attitude be gratitude*. Awed by this response, I counted backwards from five to one, slowly opened my eyes and closed the case, wondering had I drifted too far into solitude. And now I began to wonder was I entering into solitary confinement like most serious writers, or was I becoming too obsessed with silent thought?

6

"Longing is, for most of us, an essential stage in spiritual life." February, 1997

Solitary confinement? I whispered to myself, rising from the recliner to open the blinds and let the break of daylight peep inside, then hurrying to turn up the sound on the intercom...Was my longing for spiritual understanding leading me into solitary confinement?

Undoubtedly, it was. But I was enjoying every moment of it

until I paused to stare at a newspaper clipping from my research folder to find love expressed through kindness and concern, an insight that would help my attitude be gratitude.

Because of free will, my peaceful mind was now shattered by the newsclipping of Palestinian militants suicide bombings and other attacks on Israelis while I was trying to type about the joy of loving one's neighbors. The news reports told how Israeli soldiers stormed one of the holiest sites in Islam immediately after noon prayers. Months ago, I recalled *The Herald* had read: "Say a prayer for prayers" amid the anger and bloodshed because dozens were dying over boundaries *Genesis* set forth. Wasn't this a follow-up of *Genesis*? Was this a result of free will?

Newsclippings from *The Herald* also highlighted the release of a long-lost Atom-Bomb grotesque footage of Hiroshima, Japan detailing the awesome killing of over 200,000 people. I again thought about Adam and Eve (atom and evil) and wondered was this a coincidence or was the universe sending us a message.

I thought about the bloody Korean War that left my husband and other veterans totally disabled. And I thought about free will, now recalling a question I had humbly asked Mother Nature in our second book: *If the universe is unfolding as it should, and everything is determined, and the laws of science are the expression of the will of God, can 'a theory of everything' ever let us know what is determined?*

As I was pondering that question, I thought about those reports that poured from WSVN-Channel 7 in the wake of jury selection for the O.J. Simpson civil suit a few months ago, and how carefully they were picking a jury of O.J.'s peers...which meant he was Mr. Multicultural. The media's serious concerns about domestic violence had become nationalized in the light of the Simpson Trial, even though multi-media was sensationally reporting only one fraction of the violence that is dominating the universe.

Before I could question "why?"... another newspaper clipping caught my eyes: "*Ex-skinhead now teaches tolerance to kids*." I read with even more seriousness about the conference in which more than 500 religious and community leaders were expected to attend. The conference would focus on hate in America and on issues of Black-Jewish relationships.

There's a long roster of experts lined up to talk about hate and intolerance at a Miami conference next week sponsored by the Simon Wiesenthal Center and Florida Memorial College.

One of them knows hate better than the rest. Thomas Leyden, of Southern California, beat so many people bloody in the name of racism, he lost counting.

Leyden, 30, lived 15 years of his life in the grip of the neo-Nazi movement. On October 10 at Miami's Crown Plaza Hotel, he will talk about how he managed to free himself , at a conference titled "Stemming the Tide of Intolerance."

Leydon was a goose-stepping big-boot-wearing skinhead with all the tattoos to prove it. Then one day, about a year ago, he was watching TV with his 3-year old son, and the kid said something about the 'niggers" on the screen.

Something snapped in Leyden.

"I started looking at him as me 12, 13 years down the road. And I didn't like it. I thought, "Oh my God, he's not going to be a doctor or anything. He's going to be beating people for no good reason. Then I started thinking, 'Why are you doing this?'"

...Leyden now teaches kids to resist neo-Nazi tactics and how to combat hate.

The interesting article spoke at length about Leydon. Amazed at the courage of this young ex-Marine who came forward from a close-knit Irish-Catholic family to reveal his story, I said to the universe... "Leyden has discovered from his life experiences that love finds expression through kindness and concern. We can all learn this lesson of sharing from our life experiences because conversation enriches the understanding.

"But why is it so difficult for us to understand it?"

"Why DO YOU think it's so difficult for man to understand how to love one another?" the universe asked, witfully responding to my question with a question to let me know that the answers to all my questions are within me.

Then, following a brief silence, it continued: "The heart knows the answer and can give you all the information you need. The heart is all-wise."

A pensive silence swelled. I wanted to ask the universe was it the Creator's will that I ask the questions?. Then, recalling my scholarly husband's once-upon-a-time statement that perhaps God should have never allowed man free-will to do his own thinking, I wondered about the comment, about its tactful sense of humor.

It didn't sound like humor to me anymore, although I needed a good laugh. I laid the newspaper clippings aside and decided to return to the joyful feelings of love.

But then I was back into *Genesis* again. There was no getting away from those guys that gave us our roots! Oh well...I continued to thumb through the research folder.

Pausing, I thought about how peaceful the bag lady might be, and that perhaps she was a writer trying to understand an experience like The Trial of the Century. I thought about the multi-talented, nationally known Japanese writer Kenzaburo Oe, the 1994 Nobel literary laureate who said that his creative works and his child with severe disabilities saved him from being destroyed by depression, alcohol, political torment and suicidal temptations. Yes, love for his talent and his child saved him, he admitted, then added: "I do not believe in God but sometimes I want to say, 'thank you.'" At first, after reading his last statement, I was stunned. "All these marvelous blessings he's been given, and he doesn't believe in God?" I whispered, appalled. "How ungrateful!"

But then the universe peacefully whispered back, "God is love. Only mature minds can grasp the simple truth in all its nakedness." I nodded and smiled, "Thank you, 'LOVE,' for being Kenzaburo

Oe's courageous spirit in the midst of his pain and suffering! Thank you, 'LOVE,' for making him a channel of your genius! And, thank you, 'LOVE,' for helping me to grasp the simple truth in all its nakedness by being in the pristine state."

I love reading Oe's books because he writes out of pain and passion. An article about his life said that "Isolation is the overarching theme of his whole existence, the quality that has made him Japan's great chronicler of exquisite pain." The article stated that he would be reading from his book at the Miami Book Fair International that November. I had hoped that John and I would be there to hear him but John's bedsore, at that time, was keeping him bedridden. Doctor's orders. Too bad, the trial of the Century Part 2 wasn't on TV.

Like Kenzaburo Oe's life, most of the lives of outstanding personalities I have studied are people who have undergone tremendous suffering. I wondered about John and my life when I realized that their talents grew out of separation, isolation, bereavement, depression, chronic illness and other experiences. In 1949 O.J. had rickets. His mother made home-braces with a bar. He wore them until he was five years old. The courage of the human spirit was molded in his childhood.

"Depression?" I shrieked, pulling another article from the folder that spoke of depression as oftentimes being fatal._*And now I yearned to go into the kitchen and bake a batch of Duncan Hines Deluxe Brownies* and share them with the bag lady near the corner of 117th Street. Perhaps she and I could sit and talk about the civil trials.

I gladly went to the kitchen to bake them. And even as I was stirring the brownie mixture, my thoughts were being stirred by past events faster than my hand-stroking the blended ingredients of oil, eggs and water.

Pouring the brownie mixture into the 12x17 inch stainless steel baking pan and placing it in the oven, I thought about the talented poet, Ann Baxter, and her oven suicide. Then recalling my husband's warning about the cause/effect of too much depression, I by-passed Baxter and thought about writer Rudyard Kipling.

Feeling like the black sheep who had lost its way, I thought about Kipling whose early deprivation and unhappiness had a profound effect upon his future In his story "*Baa Baa Black Sheep,*' Kipling gave an autobiographical account of a dreadfully unhappy part of his life, referring to his mental suffering as calculated torture. "Waiting while the civil jury is delibrating is the epitome of mental suffering and calculated torture," I said to the universe.

Even this darn wired brassiere I'm wearing and that's hurting hell outta me is mental suffering and calculated torture, my thoughts said into the 350-degree oven that badly needed cleaning with my Amway Oven Cleaner. "Residue wipes away without heavy scrubbing," I recalled my up-line saying, and suggesting that I needed the cleaner because its convenient aerosol formula lifts grease and baked-on foods like my spilled brownie mix.

"Depression?" I kept hearing myself whispering into another voice that kept whispering as I closed the oven door. "Is the jury still deliberating? I'm hurting!"

"*Alice, I want you to stop being obsessed with those trials. That's why you're hurting and experiencing writer's block. Find something constructive to do and clean up your house! Frankly, you should be writing. And another thing, why don't you take off that wired uplift piece of nylon with its elastic section, nylon & spandex? Haven't you heard that those wired bras can cause cancer?*"

"This wired bra can cause breast cancer?" I said to whoever said that to me. Ignoring the paranoid comment, I turned my attention back to the subject of depression and the civil jury's torturous waiting, and began mixing another batch of brownies for the bag lady whom I was beginning to envy. After all, I might be joining her soon if O. J. is found financially liable for the deaths.

Feeling more depressed than ever, I said to the universe: "To me it seems that the American system has a built-in mechanism to keep Black men under control...to kill them, if possible, or to jail them to lengthy periods, or to break them financially. Why?"

> *Where cross the crowded ways of life*
> *Where sound the cries of race and clan*
> *Above the noise of selfish strife*
> *We hear Thy voice, O Son of Man.*

Although the universe had answered, I still needed more answers so I continued making brownies. There's something about chocolate that tranquilizes. Nature made chocolate that way. There was enough deluxe mixture in the family-size box to make seventy medium 2x2 inch brownies and somebody happy and/or fatter. After envying Oprah Winfrey's weight loss and fighting to stay in my size tens, I had formed a habit of baking them and giving them all away to wonderful friends instead of eating them all myself (like the Nutty Professor). I especially gave them to the kind, skinny nurses at VA; my talented skinny graphic artist and his devoted staff, and the various church ministries engaged in fundraising projects to help the needy. I call that kind of work being constructive.

This habit of baking brownies, although humorously two-fold in its purpose, had become a depression buster for me.

Enjoying the baking and still wondering why are writers often depressed, I thought about Edward Lear whose nonsense rhymes and comic drawings have entertained both adults and children for over a hundred years. Lear was prone to depression which was further complicated by epilepsy throughout his life.

"Depression?" I again repeated, cracking six eggs and dropping their contents into the mixture, wondering which came first, the chicken or the egg.

Laughing and still humbly admitting that I often write and bake brownies to ward-off bouts of depression, I assumed that this could be a part of Mother Nature's plan to help me put bad habits to good use.

Continuing in thought as I stirred the mix, I recalled my therapy treatments. Therapy revealed that I've suffered with depression most of my life. Wow! It revealed that I humbly moved through life like a shadow, creating my own world of fantasy in the struggle to survive (synonymous with Darwin's theory: *survival of the fittest*). I later discovered the truth of this statement in my solitude, being haunted with painful memories of sudden deaths of loved ones, chronic illnesses of loved ones, fatal accidents of loved ones, pain and suffering of loved ones, especially peers. Perhaps if I didn't love the loved ones as the Creator had commanded us to do, the tragedies wouldn't have pained me.

I recalled when I was ten-years-old and the farm horse ten-year-old Calvin Shaw was riding from the tobacco field became frightened and sped off like a frightened, race horse. He threw Calvin off his back and brutally dragged him nonstop all the way from the field, through the two-mile Leila Thicket, and into the stall where he stood and innocently awaited his master whose mangled, bloody body now dead dragging beneath, his left leg twisted in the curb reins.

Calvin was our next door energetic neighbor and an overactive, restless schoolmate. Older folks said he was an abused child. I distinctly remembered for years every detail of the front yard funeral and the mournful death hymns sung by adults that cried throughout the restless March winds as we viewed his distorted face, lying on a white, ruffled satin pillow of the white casket. For years, it seemed nothing could dry away our childhood memories and tears. For years, it has been my firm belief that deaths and funerals can have a lifelong psychological effect on little children if they aren't given proper counseling.

I rested my thoughts and checked the brownies in the oven. They looked good, smelled good, and made me feel good to be giving them to my dear friends who loved brownies; and especially to the nice bag lady.

After removing the pan of baked brownies from the rack, I immediately slid in the second pan and returned to more thoughts of childhood that focused episodes of kindness and concern in my world while I busily cleaned the white kitchen cabinets, refrigerator and stove...not the oven, you guys... with my Amway products.

I remembered that in an effort to accept painful experiences in life such as death...which is so final... I memorized practically every inspirational hymn in the Baptist Standard Hymnal that dealt with worship and praise. I loved being in love with the universe. It is a peace that surpasses all understanding. One day I'll learn to "let go and let God" because, perhaps the universe is unfolding as it should. It would be nice if the universe would give us humans "a theory of everything" to let us know what is determined. What's all this talk about cloning humans? Perhaps one of those cloned humans will have some logical answers.

Being shattered by pain was something I often faced because I had a genuine love for all nature and enjoyed writing about the universe, unaware that love can be painful as well as joyful. Loving one's neighbor can be painful because we hurt when they hurt. We love Jesus and the churches are still guiding us to be pained by his suffering and death, and for good reason. It makes us humble. And in feeling humble we, like little children, can truly feel the joy of love.

I recall the Christmas season when I was a little girl and my loving, very religious father shot Nellie in the head, right between the eyes. Nellie stood humbled like an innocent little two-year-old, peering into that gun barrel without flinching. "Bang!" And Nellie fell to the ground. She was my favorite little precious piggy; and I had grieved the entire six months she had been in the fattening pen. When she was barbecued, I couldn't touch her meat, and it seemed I couldn't stop crying. I felt at one in the heart of all creation.

I also recalled that decades later, and while hurriedly dressing for school and sharing the incident with my husband, John, he said: "I'll never forget the Easter when my father killed my pet bunny rabbit, too, and I couldn't stop crying. But you must remember, Alice, that Mother Nature made all meat..including yours...for somebody's dinner. You weren't eating the pig's soul. That belongs to eternity... the Creator."

I had shrieked, "Pigs don't have souls, John!"

He then answered, "You don't know that because you don't recall ever being a pig, Alice."

Undaunted, I fought back: "Sometimes I eat like one!"

And then he tactfully dropped his bombshell: "Mother Nature doesn't let pigs overeat like us 'free-will' humans, She takes care of her children and their eating habits even when we humans try to fatten them up for ourselves to eat. Then we overeat all that greasy pork, knowing that the meat causes all kinds of illness, and even finally killing us so the worms can feast on our meat, or at least what's left of it after former worms ate us to our deaths. We humans with our 'free wills' sometimes make the wrong choices and Nature never forgives, even though she creates these hideous instincts in us, her children."

"But John," I had tearfully said after listening to his disturbing truths, "Nature blessed all her children with the gift to love. We're told to love, but when we love, strife arises; and we're told that that's the story and glory of love. Descartes said that for the sake of something no one loves, strife never arises, there's no pain if it perishes, no envy if it's possessed by someone else, no fear, no hatred, no commotions of the mind at all...for all these are the consequences only of the love of things that're perishable."

"Then, fall in love with love. It's not perishable; it's eternal!" he had staunchly said before snatching his briefcase from the desk to hurry off to his University of Cincinnati classes.

God is love!, I had thought to myself, then dropped my hair wig and ran behind him, yelling my response to his back: "John, I now understand what Descartes meant when he said that the love toward an ethereal thing and infinite alone feeds the mind with pleasure, and it's free from all pain, so it's much to be desired and to be sought out with all our Might!"

Astounded by my response, John had raised his hand in midair and made a victory sign. "Love is eternal!" he said.

Seeing this, I applauded my teaspoon of understanding and thanked the Creator for writers like Descartes. Pausing, I had wanted to ask the Creator why didn't he let Jesus of Nazareth write his own philosophy that love is expressed through kindness and concern instead of leaving it up to those disciples who probably misinterpreted much of Jesus's teachings...especially Matthew 10:14 and verses 34-37.

And now, looking back on the unfolding events and accepting the universe's usual response to all of my questions with its: *Since love is the only answer, what then is the question?* I was beginning to listen more pensively to the tiny voice inside. With humility and in solitude, I continued enroute to the Holy Grail, my favorite song sounding in the quietness of my higher consciousness.

With deeds of love and mercy the heavenly kingdom comes.

My mind steered me back into the subject of depression, undoubtedly for the purpose of clarifying my own bouts with the mysterious little invader.

I thought about poets who suffered from recurrent episodes of depression such as Christopher Smart, John Clare, Gerard Manley Hopkins, Anne Sexton, Hart Crane, Theodore Roethke, Delmore Schwartz, Randall Jerell, and Robert Lowell. Clare and Smart were admitted to madhouses; Crane, Jarell and Sexton all committed suicide.

"But they were still writing?" I said to the universe as I washed the cabinet shelves, After all, it was the universe that suggested that I clean house, whatever it meant by that. "Why did you let this misfortune happen to these talented writers?"

Reminiscing about the pain and suffering of individuals who later became writers led me to wonder about the theory of free will. This insight also enabled me to realize that writing is not a profession but a vocation of unhappiness!

What a discovery! Then why can't I write about my unhappiness with these trials?

Searching and longing for answers within a suffering society that believed in free will, and fully aware that longing is an essential stage of spiritual growth, I wondered why was I yet seeking when I truly believed that we act only from the Creator's will?

In the search for answers, I was reminded of the theory that man needs difficulties because they are necessary for health.

Aware of this, I agreed with the universe, and said, mounting the mini-ladder to reach a higher shelf, "John and I enjoy writing for health reasons. And we, like other writers, feel compelled in pursuit of virtue to share our writings in ways that'll be beneficial to others, and in a healthful, cyclical way, bring benefit back to us as we gain wisdom, knowledge and understanding in our worlds of solitude! So why am I experiencing writer's block? I should be writing about my playmother, domestic violence, wife abuse. Why are you letting O.J. take up so much of our space? Is this also a choice? He and all the lawyers and witnesses are quite interesting. Are they your body? Thank you for sharing these dual experiences, although your universal message is almost too deep for us to understand."

The silence told me that these questions are fine as long as we embrace the spirit of love.

Again I agreed, then continued to wonder about free will, recalling how the prophets said that God hardened Pharaoh's heart when Moses was trying to free the Hebrews. "Did he harden O.J.'s heart if he is guilty of those murders?

"Don't let this brutal thing be true. Help us find who did this to your lovely angels. Had your angels completed their journeys when you took them away? For some reason, I feel strongly that they had completed their journeys, and now they are going to help us with ours by shining their light into our lives. There are too many mysteries going on whenever I meditate to you about them and the pain that keeps twisting in my heart. When you bring their faces to my higher consciousness, there's such a calm and peaceful feeling that surrounds me, filling the universe like the morning sunshine. Then, when I come out of meditation and hours later, allow my mind to be swept into the brainwashing reports of the trials, there is so much strife. I'm frightened. What is the universal message? If it's love, then what's with this racial intervention? To show us the power of its evil?

"Can you help us understand this whole nightmare that's driving me practically nuts trying to read your universal message so that we can answer your call? If I could write about it, the therapy would certainly restore me to sanity. With all this Christian faith, why can't I write about it? Perhaps you feel I should be universal, highly respecting all religions. I heard that the Internet is going to have a world without religious doctrines. Is this free will? Help?"

"Oh boy," I whispered, stealing a phrase from John's vocabulary. "Why am I searching for understanding when even the various religions can't come to an agreement about free will?"

In response to my question, I recalled the modern Indian sage Ramana Maharshi's definition that a genuine seeker is someone who has a passionate longing to break free from life's sorrows... not at all by running away from them, but by growing beyond his mind which knows neither birth nor death and by experiencing in himself the reality of the self.

"There's your answer, Alice," I said to myself, climbing higher on the mini step-ladder to wipe clean the top shelves. "And just as John often says...when we believe that everything is the Creator's will, that perception stops conversation!"

Case closed, I said to myself, still wondering whose will it was that kept me questioning my mind. Could it be cause and effect? Throughout our marriage I had been listening to my husband who believed in thinking deeply. Perhaps that was one of the causes that triggered his MS.

"Who knows?" I asked, now cleaning the shelves of the refrigerator and wondering why did the quiet voice tell me to clean up my house. It looked pretty clean to me. I need to go and join the bag lady.

Philosophy has always been John's favorite subject. He had said that philosophy tries to give people a unified view of the universe; and that it also seeks to make a person become a more critical thinker by sharpening his ability to think without confusion in our complicated world.

"Man thinks with his mind," I said to the spirits of philosophers. "Lizards think with their minds, and when a lizard is killed, his tail continues to wiggle several minutes after the kill. Where is the mind located, Mr. Philosopher?"

Minutes later and in the midst of whispers that kept saying "God is the mind with which we think," I thought I smelled something burning.

"My brownies!" I screamed, snatching open the oven door. They were ruined. Disgusted that I was too engrossed in thought to remember the brownies being baked, I shut off the oven, finished cleaning the kitchen, then decided to go for a walk in Miami's Coral Reef Park. I needed to let my questioning mind listen to the sounds of nature in an atmosphere of quietness and tranquility. But on the other hand, my mind told me that the worst solitude is to be destitute of sincere friendship, and to call my girlfriend, Dee, to meet me in the park for our usual five-mile walk.

But then realizing that an inner world of fantasy exists in every human being, and finds expression in an infinite variety of different ways; and that writers have a unique gift of creating their own fantasies, I ignored my intuition because I loved solitude, and I figured that kind of ludicrous thinking was for the birds.

7
"Conversation enriches the understanding."
Sunday, February 2, 1997

"'*If Birds are Free*,.. a novel.. by Evelyn... Wilde ...Mayerson, author of Sanjo,'" my John said, reading the title of the book I had handed him. I had just come from morning mass and had been talking with members of our MS support group about the lecture that was held here at the medical center three days ago. The lecturers had talked about the treatment and management of MS.

We could write another book on that mysterious stranger I had told him as I, in my over-excitement, spoke of the estimated 300,000 Americans with MS and how 30% would be confined to a wheelchair in another ten years.

"How sad," he said softly.

"The lecturers talked about the symptoms: decreased vision, tremors, weakness, balance problems, spasticity, bladder problems, ataxia, numbness."

"I've experienced all that, sweet baby."

I knew he had, but I went on naming the symptoms anyway as though needing someone to talk with. I talked about MS's urinary tract infections, personal, marital and social problems; and that the illness leads to severe disability. I even added his bedsore to the list.

Acting surprised, he teased, "I didn't know all that!!"

We had a good laugh together.

Earlier, we had been talking about Patty and how her enlightened life had led me into a world of philosophical research. John told me that if the young lady's life was sending me too deep in thought that I was burning up brownies, perhaps I should see it in light of its eternal message blended in with life experiences, like the Simpson criminal and civil trials or the book I was reading.

"I love that book," I said, tugging at my ankle-length, tightly fitting red dress with side split by designer Thomasz Starzewski, and complaining that the dress' " too-tight size ten" not being a true size ten like other designers size tens that were not too tight.

"Brownies," my husband said but I shook my head and applauded my "one-day-at-a-time" control, telling him that I needed to resume walking in the park. He agreed.

Pointing to the book, I continued: "John, sweetheart, the author, Dr. Mayerson, was my creative writing professor at the University of Miami. Don't you remember the book?"

"Sure,... I remember.. the story!. Didn't you... enjoy reading... *Sanjo* as well?"

He was concerned about the main character in *If Birds are Free*. It seemed he was aware that I wanted to identify with her, an interesting, serious thinking and intelligent bag lady named Hester.

I smirked, then moved to the opposite side of his hospital bed.

"*Sanjo's* quite interesting, but Hester's far more interesting to me," I said, rubbing my palms together. "I love Hester."

"Why?"

It seemed he was playing innocent, then later admitted that he was worried about me and my obsession with being alone. He said I needed balance.

"Balance?" I asked, then took the book from his hands and began reading from the inside cover: "'In *If Birds are free* the author of *Sanjo* has chosen a most unlikely heroine, surrounded her with a marvelously offbeat cast, added an appealing love story, and created a funny, wise, and touching novel about the survival of the weakest.'"

"'The... survival... of the... weakest,' hum?" he said, as though now understanding why I found the character interesting. He felt that multiple sclerosis had weakened our lives and made us identify with the survival of the weakest.

Laughing at his true perception, I said, "Once I remembered dreaming I was a bag lady when we were wrestling with your illness and going through all the crises of a nervous breakdown. And when I told Dr. Kensinger, my analyst, he strongly suggested that I forget that dream and focus on always having a healthy, alert mind. He suggested that I develop friendship with other people, talking and sharing present and past events with them; laughing and exploring thoughts and feelings with them."

"Dr. Kensinger was trying... to help you... keep your ...sanity," he said, then asked for his eyeglasses so that he could flip through the pages of the book with the right hand that was still doing what it ought to be doing...helping him survive with this mysterious stranger that has boldly taken over our lives.

Again I laughed, handing him the glasses and pointing to a section of the inside cover. "Listen to this, sweetheart, Hester 'might be just another 'crazy' wandering unnoticed through the urban half-life. But she commands attention."

"You'd better learn... to read to enjoy the... story without letting... yourself become... attached to... personalities,... Alice," he warned. "The book's for entertain...ment, not for you to... identify... yourself with."

"But she was a school teacher like many of us, John!" I stopped talking, then tears filled my eyes.

Worried by my tears, he ordered, "Stay outta... her world,... Alice!"

I got out of Hester's world and began talking about The Trial of the Century. I told him that I was sorry that the Simpson's civil trial was not shown on TV. My husband said that he was glad for my sake because I was taking it too seriously.

Teary eyed, I began talking nonstop. "Remember when you were a school teacher and you had MS symptoms and falling up and down stairs trying to get to your classes and folks thought you were on drugs and your principal tried to fire you and you were so frustrated and confused with the universe 'cause the universe wasn't hearing our prayers and you almost lost your mind and you started to run away to Dayton, Ohio and be a vagabond like that other teacher who was a preacher and used to watch your sexy pictures and he ran away and his wife and poor little eight children didn't know where he was and you wanted to join the folks on Skidrow like he finally did and..."

"I said get out of her world, Alice!"

"But, John, she's humorous!"

He stared hard at me, and I got the message.

"Oh, I'm not about to be like her, sweetheart," I said and began pacing the room. "I'm too pregnant with the universe."

"Pregnant?"

"I got the term from Mother Teresa."

"Oh boy!" he said, further stating that the phrase was a unique way of saying she is in love with life.

Drying my eyes, I continued: "However, I like Hester's honesty, wisdom, her tactfulness, her insight, her innocence, her humility, her gratitude and all the good fruits of the spirit. She should've been a writer validating John Dewey's philosophy."

He smiled. "Maybe she was..a writer..., Alice."

"Then perhaps that's why I'm intrigued by her personality."

He removed his glasses. "You'd better be... intrigued ...with using your therapy."

Nodding my head and stretching my eyes, I said, "Oh, I'm into using my therapy every moment of the day!"

"Good!"

Lord, why am I letting my sweet man control me from his hospital bed? I silently asked the universe. My analyst had suggest that I listen to my husband's economic wisdom. I suppose I'd better continue to listen to his spiritual wisdom, too, after all, it was he who suggested that I go to an analyst in 1975 when I was totally refusing in spite of the family doctor's advice when MS was destroying the marriage.

Thinking on this and the racial tensions the trials were stirring up, I groaned exhaled, inhaled, then said nonstop:

"Frankly, John, anyone who spent almost twenty years in therapy before becoming a therapy dropout because she recently discovered that her tall handsome priestly-looking 'White -White-Whity-White therapist acting like a Great White Father' refused to voice his professional opinion about the not-guilty verdict as she requested and strongly suggested that she lighten-up on the Simpson case and stay focused on her own physical and spiritual health and her disabled husband's world should be able to understand all the various schools of thought."

He frowned and shook his head. "Don't drop out of therapy, Alice."

"Why not? Therapy has taught me to understand the various schools of thought such as Nihilism, Existentialism, Stoicism, Pragmatism, Theism, Meism."

"'Meism? ...What's Meism?"

Laughing, I slapped my hands over my chest. "Me!"

"You should be.. concerned.. about God,... nature and... society."

"I am! But when I get too deep into it, I begin to understand confused societies like Hester's, and the O.J. Simpson trials, and the prosecutors and the dependents and the witnesses and the poor little victims and..."

"But you've... gotta know... balance, Alice! It's good therapy!"

"He didn't seem to care if I dropped out of therapy. It seemed he pushed me outta therapy!"

"Maybe he's... trying to help you use your therapy..as usual...and stop drowning...yourself in chicken soup...because of Simpson's trials."

Drowning myself in chicken soup, hum? I thought to myself. Suddenly, I recalled my Atlanta University dean of education professor saying that it doesn't matter how much a person knows, but how he feels about and what he does with that which he knows is very important.

"Sweetheart, I watched the criminal trial and listen to reports of the civil trial. They're all educational. John Dewey's philosophy of *pragmatism* insisted that any experience is a part of education!"

"I agree... with... that! Using your therapy is an... education."

"Our therapy is an education," I corrected.

He agreed and smiled. "Yes-s-s-s. Even the ...long years of... experiences wrestling... with MS."

"And these trials that are putting my world on hold."

We squeezed hands. "Now, John, the Trial of the Century is a broad education! A curriculum in itself! And we're still learning from all disciplines."

"Like this.. mysterious stranger... I have."

"Yes, like MS. When I read the newsletters from the *Well Spouse Foundation*, an association of spousal caregivers, I can identify with all those caregivers. I read the newsletters over and over because they're so educational. The information on those pages lets me know that divine discontent is an inescapable part of the human condition. I'm learning, John."

"But, let's learn... peacefully, baby."

"I'd like to write peacefully, John, but how can I when divine discontent is an inescapable part of the human condition. Undoubtedly, you weren't listening to me!"

"I was listening,... Alice. And you can write... peacefully. Just... use your therapy to write your thoughts and feelings."

"I kissed his hand. "I'd rather use your brains. I miss you very much. Conversation enriches the understanding, and conversing with you has always enriched mine. We could talk about why technology is a form of life!"

"Oh boy!" He kissed my hand in return. "MS... made us... shift gears."

"Networking...Survival of the weakest,'" I said and he understood.

Still concerned, I talked about Hester, the courageous bag lady. My husband did find the story amusing. But, he didn't want me to be locked into a private world. He insisted that I use my therapy and not let feelings of racism destroy me and my respect for the analyst.. He also suggested that I continue walking in the park with my good friend, Dee, because man is a social being and needs interaction with others to find meaning in life.

"John, sweetheart, Dee and I often walk."

"I mean... in the real... world, Alice, not in... your fantasy... world. In Coral Reef Park...with friends. Not on the Internet"

Then, shaking the book at him, I said, "In this story, Hester had a warm circle of friends! Hume and Viney, they were dog-house twins who were inseparable. And then there was the Rolexman with his suitcase filled with expensive watches. I bet he was a general in the Korean War like some of those vets that live under the bridge on Northwest Tenth Street."

My husband smiled, realizing that most of the homeless men that wander the Miami streets are war veterans. "Miami... has its share of... homeless."

We talked about the armed forces and how the government is taking care of its veterans even though my husband was only getting ten percent compensation for his total disability which flared up while he was in Korea. He expressed his gratitude for being at VA and the professional medical care he was receiving.

"One of the social workers said you should be getting one-hundred percent compensation, but life isn't always fair, sweetheart," I said, myself now fighting to stay off welfare.

"No, it isn't, he said and cleared his throat. "We learn by living."

"John sweetheart, 'truth is stranger than fiction.' We write to stay afloat."

"Just tell the truth."

"But tell it with a slant... *Genesis* style," I added and chuckled. "I should write about interesting experiences from our rental apartments."

"Oh boy." He then laughed and began talking about our many learning experiences while renting our apartment buildings in Cincinnati. I recalled one of our tenants, a young, White fashion model, Pam, who used to go with a Black, handsome neurologist who'd often slap her around yelling, "I'm a mean nigger!"

I laughed and mentioned this to John, then asked, "Why did

she continue to let him into her apartment?"

"She loved him, Alice."

Groaning, I shook my head and thought about the song sung by blues singer Billie Holiday: *My man is evil sweet as he can be, but I can't quit 'cause he's so good to me...He beats me in the morning but he knocks me out at night.*

"Love is strange," I whispered, wondering did Pam's father beat her mother or did O.J. see his angry father strike his loving, Christlike mother.

Thinking about domestic abuse, I recalled another attractive, young couple, Joy and Tony Lovette, who lived in one of our apartment buildings on Euclid Avenue in Cincinnati, Ohio. Some of the curious tenants in the building said the couple belonged to a religious cult called Heaven's Gate. Joy Lovette was a brilliant university student who worked part-time for wealthy Jews who lived in Bond Hill. Tony was a science and math teacher. According to Joy, she and Tony were fed up with a world of racism and violence and felt the planet earth was corrupted with violence and many humans were fallen angels like the archangel, Lucifer. Like Jesus' teachings, Joy and Tony would talk interestingly about the Kingdom of Heaven where there is no violence, sickness or death. When I told them that the Kingdom of Heaven is within us, they said that the Kingdom of Heaven is within our spirits, and that our spirits are housed in our bodies. They said that the spirit is eternal but the body is not; and that we, like Adam and Eve, were born into the spirit of love and service; and like Adam and Eve, we earthly humans allowed Lucifer, the serpent, to control our lives. For this reason, we are a corrupted planet of people whose minds are locked into violence. They said that Jesus was from the evolutionary level above human and we are to be loving and nonviolent like him.

Being a Korean War veteran who fought for his country, my husband felt insulted by Tony's accusation that we are corrupted. When he told Tony this, he understood because he himself had been in the Vietnam War. Tony implied that humans are so accustomed to maintaining the external order of life by violence that they cannot conceive of a life being possible without violence. When John asked Tony did he and Joy belong to a religious cult, Tony replied with frankness, "All religions are cults." Shattered by this frank response, John and I trembled with fear, but were determined to follow Jesus' teachings insasmuch as The Prophet Paul said in Ph. 2:12-13:...*work out your own salvation with fear and trembling for it is God which worketh in you*.

I recalled Tony saying that one man's cult is another man's religion, and that the big four religions of the world are just a form of worship with political power because politics control everything. John told him that the Creator controls politics and everything and that's why we all needed to let go and let God. Tony and Joy were computer geeks who perhaps did let go and let God.

And now staring at John and realizing that the only truth we know is that we do not know, I began talking about tenants Joy and Tony, who according to Joy's parents, were now living happily in San Francisco.

"Oh boy," my husband said. "They've always believed in the magic of love."

Then squeezing John tightly and kissing his golden cheek (slightly smeared with Capsaicin cream, we later learned) I left the room with my lips on fire, snapping my fingers and singing: *Under That Old Black Magic Called Love*, still clutching my favorite book, *If Birds Are Free*.

CHAPTER FOUR

Jesus said: "Blessed are those who have chosen their solitude, for they will find the kingdom of heaven."
-The Gospel of Thomas (lst-2nd Century)

FEBRUARY, 1997

Birds fluttered amid evergreens as I walked briskly along the paved pathway of Coral Reef Park the following Monday morning, inhaling and exhaling nature's cool breezes filled with the freshness of quiet day. My body felt fresh and lightweight in the red and white adidas top and fitness shorts I was wearing.

It was sunny , February 3. And children chatted on their way to school, laughing and enjoying the friendship of each other. Their presence and laughter reminded me of my own childhood and my playmother who I thought was a very unusual girl and was deeply impressed by her spiritual concern for other people. She used to give me beautiful boxes of handkerchiefs.

Thinking about Patty always made me think about the trials and the deceased victims. Frustrated, I wanted to escape from both; but I couldn't because there were two different important issues at stake here; and I loved all three individuals involved. They were beautiful spirits of love. The jury was still deliberating the civil case. I, too, was deliberating on whether I should be waiting to exhale or inhale my "Thy Will Be Done."

And now as I walked through the park listening to the chatter of young voices, I kept remembering Patty's kind personality. When I had told my hospitalized husband of Patty's return visits in my dreams and how suddenly she had died when I was six, he smiled and said: "Angels like her don't die, Alice; they just come to bring a message from our Creator and then fly back home."

Thinking on this and about my deceased grand nephew and niece who were now with the angels, I smiled, enjoying children sounds and the birth of new day. I was peacefully awaiting its many surprises to be painted by my own thoughts and feelings amid the confusion as to where were we going, technologically, as a civilization. Perhaps I needed to take my mind off Patty's message for a while because a part of me was beginning to embark on a deep search for some serious answers regarding solitude in times of depression.

"The book of *Genesis* showed us that man makes his own heaven or hell by his thoughts and feelings; this is the law of cause and effect...the law of the subconscious mind," I whispered to myself, walking briskly across the bridge as ducks swam in the running stream, quacking their friendly chatter to one another.

I mimicked their quacking, and heard the envisioned voice behind me giggling.

"Alice Johnson, I know you wobble but I didn't know you quacked, too," Dee said, her index finger lightly pushing into my left arm.

"Dee!" I said with stretched eyes, giving a usual bear hug to her medium built figure, then complimenting her neatly shaped curly perm and staring at the paper bag she was carrying. "What'cha' got there, girl?"

"Oh, just something for the ducks and their little ducklings," she replied, removing her sunglasses and placing them in the pocket of her Reebok white and red nylon warm-ups.

Dee was the fiscal officer for John and my production company. We would be in production at the Joseph E. Caleb Auditorium on Friday, February 7 to present our musical docudrama in celebration of Black History Month and emphasizing multicultural education.

She and I talked about the performance which was only four days away as I watched her feed the ducks. Chantal Legros, director and choreographer would be doing the show with her Danzare International artistic performers.

I wiped my shades. "Once upon a time I used to feed the ducks, but then I stopped. My world has been put on hold."

"When did you stop? After Sally died in a diabetic coma?"

"Yes! " I said sadly. "And knowing my Sally, she's probably up there asking, 'Lord, what am I up here after?'" When Dee laughed, I continued, "Sally said I was getting far too obsessed with the brother's real-life soap opera."

"Aren't we all? And now we're sitting on edges waiting for the all White civil jury's verdict. But we're not letting it stop us from living our own lives."

"Oh, it's not stopping my life. It has slowed me down considerably, but I did manage to get those invoices to the schools that are bringing busloads of students to the auditorium for the play on Friday. I'll need you and Bankston to help 'cause I'm wrestling with a load of confusions. "

"Plus all this frustration about the two trials...a criminal trial and a civil trial. The law states that a person who is found not guilty of a crime cannot be tried a second time. Not guilty means not liable, not responsible, not accountable. Actually, what do you think about all this?"

"I don't know what to think. They're going through the evidence with a fine tooth comb. I'm just as frustrated as you are."

"Well, let's hope the county's moving forward in race relations instead of moving backwards."

"Something within me seems to be dying, especially after Sally died."

"Tell me about Sally's death, Alice. Ethel said Sally didn't even know she had diabetes, and that it seems something within you died with her."

"Something within me was dying before she died. And she kept warning me to get off the Simpson case because I was turning it into a mental institution. I told her there was something about the case that's very disturbing."

"That's because it seems to be dividing the races, Alice, and you're into multicultural education. It is very disturbing! And what makes it so horrible is that the whole world is seeing this. I had to back away myself, especially when they got that all White jury for the civil trial with the exception of one."

I exhaled. "Yeah. This civil jury has nine Whites, one Hispanic, one Asian American and a Jamaican immigrant who describes himself as Black."

"Are they're supposed to be his peers? Since he's multicultural, Alice, they probably are." When I smiled, she continued, "Let's change the subject and wait until the verdict comes in. So, now tell me about Sally's death."

Using my therapy to ward-off deeper depressions, I quickly said, "But, let's not talk about our Sally who's now in paradise, thanks to the universe. She's probably walking along with us in her tranquil state of peacefulness which we all envy. Let's talk about you, Dee!"

"Well, you certainly have a peaceful attitude about death. Are you okay?"

"Dee, the tragedy of life isn't death; it's what we let die within us. So, lets hold on to love in a world that seems be becoming divided."

"Let's hope not."

"I'm afraid these trials are awakening me to the truth of it. It seems they're not concerned about finding the real killer or killers of those two innocent people."

"Alice, you can't worry about that?"

" Anyway, it's great to see you! Are you walking alone?"

"Well, since you're becoming so locked into your literary

world, I walk with other friends. And we talk, as usual, about things of interest to us."

"That's great! Talking with a friend, Dee, is nothing else but allowing yourself to think aloud."

She laughed. "Is that why you stay glued to that computer while John's in the nursing home? According to you, writing is nothing else but allowing yourself to think aloud." She threw some crumbs to the group of quacking Cayugas ducks.

"It's sorta like talking to myself, Dee. But my analyst said it's all right for me to talk to myself as long as I don't answer for the person with whom I'm supposed to be talking."

"But you often do, don't you? Just then, you were even talking back to you for the ducks."

"Fantasizing, I listen to the ducks spirit and converse with them. This is what we call communicating on the websites...networking."

She gulped. "What on earth are you? Some kind of mystic or something?"

"Perhaps. And I'm leaning toward some areas of Pantheism. Walking in this huge, beautiful, landscaped park I'm filled with feelings of awe and wonder of the overwhelming beauty and power of the universe."

"What on earth is Pantheism, Alice?"

"Dee, Pantheism holds, and I quote, 'that God is not necessarily a personal deity, but rather is immanent in the natural workings of the universe.'"

"You keep up that foolishness and you'll soon be excommunicated from the Catholic Church."

"I've a spiritual appreciation for technology. I feel it's God's plan."

Dee groaned. "You'd better stay off that Internet."

We both laughed, then paused as she threw a handful of bread crumbs to another gathering of quacking ducks that were wobbling toward us.

"Someone told me you've been into the teachings of Buddhism and Zen ever since Sally and your seventeen-year-old grand niece passed. Why, Alice?"

"Why? Are you kidding? We all have a unique spiritual mission. Haven't you read Deepak Chopra's *The Seven Spiritual Laws of Success* which, in my opinion, strongly embraces the Christian teachings of love, personal fulfillment and spiritual connectedness?"

"Not yet."

"Dee, you should read it! I was impressed with the personality of one the students in our University of Miami writing courses that meet at Borders Book Store who read it and was practicing it step by step! She was the one who insisted that O.J. is as guilty as sin and she can't see why I fail to see this."

"Maybe it's because you're hurting for O.J. and the victims, Alice."

"I most certainly am; and especially O.J.'s mother who's continuously praying a mother's prayer."

"Then you're torn between decision and indecision as to whether or not he's guilty. That alone can drive you out of your mind when all the time you've known him, he was like a mystical hero and you believe that he's not guilty."

"It's heartbeaking to even feel that he might be."

"And as far as his deceased wife is concerned, you've always said that you could identify with her as a wife being abused and I bet you're shocked like the rest of us about a nice person like Simpson abusing her."

"It was very depressing. I still can't understand why would a kind person like him abuse her. They had everything people dream of and Lord knows they loved each other when they got married. What else could he have wanted?"

"I don't know. But, like hundreds of angry husbands, he abused her and had the audacity to get on the stand and say he has 'never hit her when he was asked about the abusing. That hurt the dickens outta me! Now, Alice, that's what hurt more than anything he said 'cause it put a lot of doubt in people minds. Everybody now feels that it's gonna be absolutely crucial to the case."

I exhaled. "Painful. I still don't understand why he said that."

"It's painful if you feel that he's being framed and that some of the evidence against him was planted by some racist who's out to get him."

"I strongly feel that he didn't have time to commit those murders, Dee! You all are overlooking the time element. That's what infuriates me. Everyone who doubts his innocence is overlooking the time element! Even my nephew who is a police officer in Pennsylvania said lots of the policemen feel Simpson is guilty. He said that several of the cops who are used to working with cases that involve domestic violence called our hero a control freak."

"And your ex-husband, like some cops, was a control freak. Your lawyer made you get out of town and take nothing with you 'cause your life was far more important than all that material stuff you all bought together."

"Lord help us abused women."

"And then he stalked you for..how many years?...seventeen? Anyway, something like that 'cause I know you don't want to talk about it. It's a wonder you aren't a nervous wreck."

"I was until I entered psychotherapy. Tests showed that I was suffering with agitated depression. I had no idea I was so depressed. And then here comes this Trial of the Century stirring up all this terror and triggering a recurrence of agitated depression."

"But you're using your therapy."

"Not only am I using my therapy, I'm into *Genesis* because it gives us the story of creation and of original sin so that we can better understand man and his environment, good and evil, moral and ethical law, human behavior and its measurements. Who'd ever think that domestic violence could be such a powerful learning institution. I'm deep into the Bible and I'm learning about Zen and Buddhism."

"Your writing classmate is into Buddhism and Zen?"

"She has gone beyond that stage. She's an abused divorcee. She seems to have inner and outer balance." I hesitated, trying to clarify in my own mind exactly what I meant. "She believes that the internet...like the first printing press and like the radio and television, is God's will whereby the business of teaching moral and spiritual values can be driven forward throughout the universe. She believes that we humans are a part of nature and should not be taught that we're set above it, 'cause that darn lion sure isn't under our feet and he's a beast of the field! And reports of Florida's huge alligators that are eating our children..."

Dee groaned. "Alligators are supposed to be afraid of humans."

"Nor is that man-eating whale that '(whatsoever) passeth through the paths of the seas," I commented as Dee continued groaning about alligators.

"And Dee, my creative writing classmate seems to be in control of the forces that bring suffering into our lives. She believes in the Heaven's Gate religion. Her interest in it keeps piling higher and deeper with this so called Trial of the Century! Nature's law of life seems to be to create and devour."

We laughed heartily, as though laughing away the pain of suffering. Dee wiped the laugh-tears from her eyes. "We all have that problem of being confused, Alice; and we always will. But, it's just like your analyst said, you've no monopoly on human suffering. But sometimes we tend to feel that we have."

"And like my priest said, 'Suffering's there for spiritual and educational growth.' But, I want to be in control of how I intellectually perceive it, so I became interested in practicing the teachings of Buddhism and Yen, blending them in with Christianity and other religious teachings that offer a systematic way to see clearly and live wisely as taught by Jesus. Online religion."

"They all say the same thing...treat others as you'd have them treat you," she said, still throwing bread crumbs. "Here you are, little duckie,...chick chick chicko-o-o-o-."

"And that the kingdom of heaven is within you."

"So, where does this mysticism, online religion and Heaven's Gate School of Thought come in?"

"The discovery of *Nirvana*!"

"What's *Nirvana*, Alice?"

"The freeing of the heart of entanglement in all the conditions of the world like MS, those darn bedsores, agitated depression, death. And especially all that bloody fighting, bloody killings, race hatred and evil mess that blast from the news media everyday adding more stress to our already overly stressed lives. And all the illnesses like cancer, heart disease, multiple sclerosis, diabetes, massive bedsores... that keep us feeling depressed and scared as hell..." My wired brassiere was pinching my breast area.

Dee interrupted without moving her eyes from the ducks. "In other words, you want to be free from worry and just enjoy life like these little ducks. We're nature's children and we've gotta say: 'Thy will be done' like the little ducks."

In line with her comment, I continued. "We met Mother Nature in *Genesis* with all her '*will be done*' that keeps us all confused about creation, the beginning of evil, original sin, greed, lust, envy, hatred, delusions, jealousy, fear, doubt. Just a few months ago, dozens of people died in Israel over boundaries set forth by *Genesis*. I guess that was Mother Nature letting her will be done."

"So..."

"So, I'm weary of wrestling with endless suffering and frustration wondering what can we do as children of love to help causes and what we can't do. According to the Bible, *Genesis* is about how and why sin and suffering entered human experience and stayed there. According to the New Testament and Eastern religion, the kingdom of heaven is within us. I'm desperate to find that kingdom, but *Genesis* keeps flashing before me all this prehistoric history! And now the Hale-Bopp Comet!"

"You've been watching too much of Bill Moyers series on

Public Television." Dee chuckled, then sprinkled another handful of crumbs to the hungry ducks and suggested that we begin walking.

We did, and she began lecturing to me about Adam and Eve.

"Yeah, Alice, even Saint Augustine said that after Adam sinned, our corrupt nature was already present in the seed from which we were to spring. So, we all inherited Adam's sinfulness."

"That's why I'm anxious to see what Buddhism has to say about wisdom and compassion that can further awaken me, Dee, just as Jesus of Nazareth awakened us to an understanding of how to love God and love one another in our thirst for something eternal to believe in!"

"That was his mission."

"I know it was! And now, Christianity is the most widespread religion in the world. Why? Because it deals with a way of living and a way of believing through the power of God based on traditions and teachings!"

"And Jesus lived what he taught."

"This is true; and let's never forget that Jesus gave us the most sublime and benevolent code of morals which has ever been offered to man!"

"If you feel this way about Jesus's teachings, then why are you into Buddhism and all this mysticism and foolishness?"

"Because Jesus and Buddha have taught some powerful moral lessons that are universal and have been locked into the world's consciousness for thousands of years. Their teachings seem to save us from our mental and physical troubles that *Genesis* passed on to us. And the good part about it is that their disciples are still teaching these wise lessons of moral conduct."

"His name wasn't always Buddha, you know. And he lived before the birth of Jesus."

"But we aren't allowed to discuss other religions." I thought about the brainwashing we were receiving from the media about the trials. It seemed the media was highlighting Simpson's guilt and that's why most people felt he was guilty. The trials had nothing to do with being innocent or guilty. It had to do with controlling our thinking. It's no wonder I'm having problems here dealing with domestic abuse only. "And now I am confused!"

"What's wrong, Alice? Are you cracking up, or something?"

"Ever since the beginning of time, we've had trouble loving one another or treating one another with kindness and concern! And Mother Nature is to blame."

"Now, you're talking crazy. They said most writers think too hard and that's why most of 'em are weird."

With furrowed brow, I stared into space re-recalling a similar discussion in one of my university classes in which the biology professor implied that most writers, like him, find the Bible to be a series of fairy tales for teaching moral values. He had said that the Bible's mythical aspect makes it quite interesting because it focuses our selfish nature. The professor had stated that the Book of *Genesis* gave us a synopsis on the moral theme of modern society by delving head-on on the subjects of love, fear, selfishness, murder, rape, incest, adultery, child-rearing problems, family feuds, racism, environmental desecration, jealousy, rage, greed, the search for peace and search for self. I recalled my feelings of total frustrations and abandonment after hearing that discussion. It triggered the deepest state of depression I had ever known! Confused and heavyhearted, I had hurried home from class to meditate on the shock. Never had I felt so lost and lonely in my entire life because my strong belief in the Holy Bible was being torn to shreds. My life felt meaningless! When I recovered from the shock, I promised never again to let any ungodly biological scientists into my spiritual world and twist up my mind with his dogma. But now, what about the science of psychology? Would looking at the Bible from the point of psychology send me into deep states of depression because I would be gambling with my true beliefs? What a frightening way to gamble! One shouldn't tangle with his mental health, but for some reason I feel strangely propelled! Why?

"What's wrong, Alice? You look confused."

"We all should be confused and for good reason!" I said and shook my head. "We are to love one another if we are to survive!"

"Everybody knows that! So what's the problem?"

"But knowing and feeling are two different states of mind! There seems to be a conspiracy to make it difficult for us to truly love one another...even to love our own family members, brothers, sisters, relatives, friends ..husbands, wives!"

"A conspiracy?"

Then, pushing my index finger into her shoulder I said with excitement and frustration, "Dee, even psychologists have said that for one human being to love another is the most difficult task that has been entrusted to us poor ol' humans! Working with John and his negative MS personality almost drove me insane! Even though I love him dearly, sometimes his behavior would drive me absolutely crazy! If it weren't for my analyst and Dr. McAdory, Dr. Sheremata or the Well Spouse Foundation that helped me hold on to love I would've, out of frustration and anger, done what Cain did to Abel or what Joseph's brother did to him."

"What are you trying to say, Alice?"

"Loving other people is actually the ultimate task; the work for which all our other spiritual work is merely preparation! Can't you see?"

"No, I can't !"

"Frankly, I think we're naturally blind to our own human nature! We all have a selfish nature, and the roots are in *Genesis*! Buddha believes that since we've the freedom to make our own choices, we can overcome selfishness and sorrow and gain perfect freedom and peace! But our selfishness...or ego... isn't a choice. The more I think about it, the more I can see that it's inherited!"

Dee frowned. "What are you talking about, Alice? And slow down! When you get excited, I can hardly understand a word you're saying."

Speaking slower, I continued. "We learned that in *Genesis* when Cain, selfishly, killed Abel, his own brother because he was jealous when the Lord accepted Abel's offering and rejected his! We still exert this form of jealousy all over the world. We've been taught to love, but we even fail at that because of our innate selfishness...even among Christians! Can't you see?"

"Well, oftentimes we need to look out for our own selves, Alice."

"That's what these trials are teaching us all. We're missing the psychological aspects of the whole book that tells us how and why sin and suffering entered human experience and is staying there!"

"What are you trying to say, Alice? That you also believe according to *Genesis*, we're inclined to do wrong because we've a hereditary dark side?"

I nodded. "It seems we're accountable for Adam's sin even before we've done anything wrong! I'm gonna ask Father Dionne, Father Crowe, Father Clancy, Father Haynes and Father Byrne about *Genesis*, and get their different opinions 'cause they're experts on the subject. Although..."

Dee interrupted. "Aren't you gonna ask Sister Teresa, Sister Gibbs, Pastor Gigi Tinsley, Pastor Annie McRae, Pastor Marian Pratt, Pastor Venaka Silva..."

"Will you let me finish?" I shrieked.

"No!" she shrieked back, playfully, "'Cause you're being prejudiced by naming all males and Whitefolks!"

Believing that she wanted to help me snap out of the serious thought and laugh, I giggled, then we both folded into hearty laughter.

Silently thanking her for injecting humor into the discussion, I continued, but this time tearfully with the spirit of gratitude for religious ministers.

"But then, why not try asking the universe that knows everything?" she asked.

"It'll only say that 'since love is the only answer, what then is the question?'"

"What then is the question, Alice?"

"Just as I told you before. We know that love is the answer but knowing and feeling are two different states of being."

"Well, that's food for thought."

"My husband and I are into the world of thinking!" I said and stared at my watch. "As soon as we finish this walk, I'm gonna hurry home, shower and rush off to see him so we both can continue our research on *Genesis* and the religions of the world!"

"What for, Alice?"

"To discover facts and use them, Dee."

"Well, at least you're writing the stress outta your system and growing spiritually," she said as we approached her white Mercedes Benz. "But I think you need to back away from that computer for a while, Alice. You're getting carried away with all that serious talking with it. And stay off that religious Internet!"

"I did back away, Dee. I spent half the morning chatting with you. Besides, as president of the Women's Guild at my church, I do lots of community work. I belong to the Children's Cultural Coalition, MS Society, Delta Sigma Theta..."

"Alice, I know all that."

"I work and talk with lots of interesting people!"

"I'm sure you do, even when they're not around."

We both laughed.

"When I arrived this morning, I heard you talking with and for the ducks. Which wasn't unusual."

"No it wasn't unusual. I felt very comfortable talking with my brothers and sisters; they are so placid and self-contained. Imagination...an enjoyable habit I learned in childhood when my playmother was killed! So, maybe it's the path that nature intends for me to follow in my quest to live for the pursuit of greater understanding." I began singing :"'Pretend you're happy when you're blue...It isn't very hard to do..'"

She turned on the ignition. "Childhood is a world of fantasy, Alice, that's why we have Disney World. It's been said that an inner world of fantasy exists in every human being. But even so, there has to be a limit."

"The interesting part about it, Dee, is that imagination makes us distinctively human. I would always tell this to my students..'enjoy using your imagination! It's beautiful! Create pictures in your mind! The mind's a treasure house!"

"As a school teacher myself, I can understand and agree with that."

"And being around interesting friends like you who enjoy talking on interesting subjects encourages creative imagination to flourish like everything!"

She chuckled. "And now I understand how friends end up in your computer," she said and we laughed.

I stared at my watch. It was 8:15 in the morning and I didn't want to be alone. "Why don't you do another round with me?"

She stared at her watch. "Why not? I've time and I can use the exercise."

While it is true that confronting and solving life's problems is a painful process which we all would like to avoid, it seemed I was beginning to enjoy suffering through the changes in order to reach a higher level of self-understanding.

And now as I was telling this to Dee as we walked to the beat of friendly chatter, she jokingly said that many writers are weird, anyway; so it was no surprise to her.

We laughed.

"Any writer who integrates traditional psychology and *Genesis* needs his head examined," she continued humorously, gripping the package of bread crumbs she carried in her left hand; her red and white jogging suit emblematized with the name of our public service sorority.

Again, we both laughed at her humor. But I felt that the joke was on me and, following the dictates of my ego, tactfully put up my defenses.

"Once upon a time, Dee, I did have my head examined for

depressions that stemmed from childhood that were awakened by the depression that stemmed from John's chronic illness. So, now when things get next to me, I use my therapy to break away."

"How strange. I've never known you to be depressed until I read your first book, *Mysterious Stranger Aboard*, You're always so cheerful and filled with life.

"Seriously?" I asked.

"I'm very serious."

Pushing aside defenses, I apologized to my mind for ego interception, then continued. "Well, I knew that I was very unhappy practically all my life until I met John who came to my rescue. My analyst said that sometimes genetic endowment interacts with circumstances to produce our states of depression. It was he who started John and me on this writing spree as therapy."

"Yea, but you shouldn't keep yourself locked into all that writing."

"Actually, the need to be alone is a neglected human need," I said, moving from the path of a four-year old riding his Ranger GT with its fold-down windshield and seat belt. "Hi, Ranger!"

His mother, on in-line skates, smiled into our smiles.

"It seems the universe has been trying to tell me for years that being alone and writing is my survival instinct, and that suffering is part of the packaged deal."

"Maybe so," she said and laughed as we continued briskly along the curved path and across the wooden bridge.

"I'm happy when I'm writing; I'm frustrated and depressed when I'm stifled."

"Well, at least you know to keep writing. I'm sure you and John have already begun writing your third book. So what's gonna be the title of it?"

She paused and I watched her throw bread crumbs to four gray and white domestic ducks that were running toward us.

"The title? 'Love finds Expression Through Kindness and Concern.'"

"That's a nice title. What made you decide to write on that

subject?"

"Several things, but particularly my childhood playmother, Patty, who used to be happily married to a guy who loved her and then he killed her. "

"That's sad! The same thing happened yesterday right here next door to us when that young, attractive, professional track student was killed by her jealous husband. They had a darling little girl and a lovely home. It's shocking!"

"People get married to live happy together. My mother taught me that happiness isn't the goal of life; good character is. So, when *The People vs. Simpson* exploded on the scene, it brought back long buried memories of wife abuse, and all the fears I thought I had under spiritual control so that I could move on with my life. I thought about what my mother said and it made a lot of sense. Then I thought about what Patty said and that made a lot of sense."

"The Simpson case is upsetting and waking up a lot of people."

"Well, it really did upset and awaken me so badly that my childhood playmother's spirit started visiting my dreams, Dee."

"Well, you've always been a mystic."

Ignoring her humor, I continued. "My childhood playmother's death reminded me of Nicole's death and all the many, many abused and battered wives and the many, many women who're still being abused and battered. In the calmness before the explosion of the Simpson trial, we used to keep the abuse and violence buried under the rugs...sort of. Then I saw it all when it exploded before me that I myself was an abused wife."

"We recognized that in your first book, Alice."

Laughing, I said with seriousness, "But, I felt it was sort of like other folks life! I thought it was a way of life for some of us couples who're unequally yoked and trying to work through the problems in spite of this! The Simpson trial...he and his wife had love, money and fame... actually made me wake up, speak up, and help stop domestic abuse so we can save our marriages and raise our children in a spiritual, loving home atmosphere. We're so in love with being married, we women don't even know when we're being abused. And when we are abused, we sweep it under the rug and run out of the marriage without trying to help fight the violence to save future generations! We all need to return to love...unconditional love!"

"So, your next book's gonna be about love?" Again she paused and began sprinkling bread crumbs as more ducks from all directions came running toward her, their web-feet moving to the beat of quacking sounds.

"Yes." I wanted to tell her that if I don't stop being obsessed with the O.J. Simpson case that's creating writer's block, the next book's gonna be about The Calm and the Strife.

"So, it's gonna be about love, hum? What's gonna be the title again?"

"'Love Finds Expression Through Kindness and Concern.'"

"That's good! But, there you go again, beating us over the head with all this talk about love."

"That's the essence of life!"

"In today's society, money seems the essence of life. I'm anxious to hear this verdict. Just hope Simpson's insurance will pay whatever they'll be asking. I'm pretty sure it'll be a guilty verdict if any of them have read Chris Darden's book."

"I read his book and Johnnie Cochran's thoroughly. Couldn't put them down. I read so long and hard last weekend, I practically ruined my eyes. They're both very informative, and educational."

"I thought they were, too. How do you actually feel about what they're saying?"

"Darden has his own opinions. Cochran spoke from a wealth of interesting experiences which I can identify with. The writing is excellent!"

"I hope that if Simpson is found liable, his insurance company will handle the cost," she said as two brisk-walking men passed us. "My mother has Prudential and do you know they had her using her dividends to buy more expensive insurances? Didn't you read about how they've been treating elderly people?"

"Yes, I saw that. John and I are victims! Lots of poor disabled seniors are victims, Dee! We senior citizens who've experienced the spiritual life should edit the phrase to read: 'The ungodly love of money is the root of all evil.' You don't *love things* and *use* people; you *love people* and use things!'"

"That's a good point, Alice, but who's listening. People don't count nowadays, money counts; and you know that for yourself. It's been that way ever since *Genesis*. It's that way all through the old Testament. Whenever God blessed anyone most times it was with riches. See how blessed Job was after his suffering? And we still see riches as the greatest blessing and the true sign of success. Life's getting to be so expensive, it's even too expensive to die nowadays."

"Speaking of death, these funeral homes are often doing-in us poor ol' senior citizens, especially when the spouse is disabled. Another form of abuse. Enough to make me lose my faith in people."

"What are you talking about now, Alice?"

"Dee, three years ago...about six months after Hurricane Andrew destroyed our home.. a fast talking, convincing sales representative from 'Simplicity Plan' of Caballero Woodlawn Funeral home pressured me into buying a VA plot for John and me, our caskets and all funeral arrangements to lock in the price which totaled a little over ten-thousand dollars. He threatened me with the fear that if I failed to purchase them, all funeral home prices were rising so high that within the next few years, our life insurance policies wouldn't be half enough to cover our funeral expenses. After he frightened hell outta me about my poor little husband in the nursing home being left behind should I die first; and all the horrible things that could happen financially that my 'poor little disabled husband' would have to take care of while these money-crazed lawyers reduce him to shreds, I consulted with the universe and signed the contract, The monthly payments were electronically withdrawn from John and my joint bank account . Then, just last week, and for the first time in the three years, the funeral home's automatic draft was returned because of insufficient funds in my checking account. Although I had made a bank deposit later that same evening, and was told by the bank that companies always re-present the autodrafts at least once, the funeral home didn't re-present its. The funeral home immediately sent me a special delivery letter threatening to cancel my contract within two days, stating that I would not be reimbursed for any of the three years of payments I had made which averaged over $5,000. The funeral home said that I could not sell my plot or caskets to anyone or get out of the contract! I was one more frustrated and angry senior citizen. I ran to the church and told Father Dionne inasmuch as over half of the church congregation and their relatives use that funeral home."

"Most of our congregation uses it, too."

"Anyway, Father Dionne called the funeral home and asked could they please re-present the autodraft at least one time just as other businesses do, because sufficient funds were now in my account. The funeral home's feisty little clerk blatantly said they DO NOT re-present autodrafts regardless of how many years a client has been with them because it is not their policy; and that I would not be reimbursed any money if they have to cancel the contract. Fearing that this same freakish incident could happen again inasmuch as I've a disabled spouse and I myself could, one day, be mentally or physically unable to handle my financial affairs, I asked could they make it their policy to re-present the autodraft to help senior citizens who might encounter a similar problem. She said they don't do that!"

"That's preposterous!"

"Even so, it seems me and my disabled husband are locked into a big piece of mess here. Anyway, they acceded to Father Dionne's request and re-presented the draft. It saved me from breaking my neck trying to reach that office amid all that rush-hour traffic."

"Thank heavens for Father Dionne."

"The priests often come to our rescue, Dee. Religion is designed to help the poor and the sick, just as you earlier said."

"The rich and the healthy don't need it," she teased.

"Two things that are sure: taxes and death."

"That's another form of rip-off used on senior citizens. I understand you and your disabled husband had been paying property taxes for twenty years even though he was totally disabled. And when, through his VA social worker, you filed the forms that exempted you from paying property taxes, the county refused to reimburse you and your disabled husband anything for all those years they collected those expensive property taxes from your pensions."

"Isn't that sad? Isn't that depressingly sad? Even the government workers have fun abusing us," I said, massaging my forehead. "Girl, we senior citizens usually get ripped off by greedy businesses from all areas... not to mention when we go for car repairs. These people have no conscience whatsoever! Even one of the companies that used to clean our swimming pool would often give us hell! Their workers were always breaking something so that John and I could pay to have it fixed again for hundreds of dollars!"

"That's 'cause they're paid on commission, Alice!"

"That's hell, Dee! That's mental abuse! And when I read about these scams in the newspapers, I can often identify with the poor victims. Sometimes I have a very difficult time talking to the universe, giving thanks and asking for guidance in dealing with its money-crazed creatures whom we're suppose to love with kindness and concern here on planet earth."

We both laughed. I removed my eyeglasses, wiping them as I continued talking. "I've a feeling that's where most of my depression comes from. I hate having to pay people money I don't owe them."

"Then maybe in a way money is the essence of life and seems

to be the universe's hidden agenda because nowadays it's getting too expensive to be born, to live and to die, wouldn't you agree?" she asked as we approached our cars.

I said "no" and added: "But we've been given some negative attitudes about money since the beginning of time. Remember the song: '*You'd Better Get a Home on That Rock*."

"Not the rock of Prudential Insurance, I hope."

"No, the rock of salvation. One of the verses of the song said: '*The rich man died when he lived so well; when he died he had a home in Hell. He had no home on that rock can't you see?*'"

"I remembered that song. We used to sing it in Sunday School!"

"And, Dee, the second verse said: '*Poor ol' Lazarus poor as I; when he died he had a home on high. He had a home on that rock, don't you see.*'"

"Brainwashed in childhood that having lots of money makes one evil. With money we can help others on this spiritual journey, It's the greed that makes one evil and corrupted, not the lack or love of money. That's why lots of hard working Christians live in poverty all their lives and pass it on from generation to generation. Someone's sending us the wrong messages."

"We've been taught that the purpose of money is to finance life, but life keeps getting more and more expensive even though we keep working harder and harder."

"Don't feel bad, even the country's in debt. I'm anxious to hear what President Clinton has to say tomorrow night in his State of the Union address."

"Do you think the jury will give us its verdict before then?" I felt a sense of depressing guilt for wanting to hear the verdict instead of the President's speech.

"That's a thought? I haven't been listening to the news. But I'm sure if the case is still on, my husband's gonna be watching the State of the Union Address because he thinks the whole Simpson case has to do with media rating. Most folks said that's why they needed to sensationalize a case like Simpson's.. a celebrity like him could generate a lot of income for the system, and high ratings for the media. High ratings mean more money. The bottom line is always the dollar. With all these huge companies engaging in downsizing, the economy is in big trouble."

"You mean politics have something to do with the case?"

"Research found that genes control our inner life just as politics and politicians control our outer life," she said, bending and touching her toes.

"I would hope not." The noise of the riding lawnmower almost drowned our voices.

"Everyone knows that politics and politicians decide the value of your money, the floor under your wages, the wars you fight, the interest you pay, the speed you drive, the taxes you pay; they control the purity of your food, the schooling of your children, the...."

Surprised and awakened, I interrupted, adding: "Yes! And we're aware that politics and politicians also hand out subsidies to airlines, oil companies, farmers, magazines, newspapers, builders, bankers, and they protect or destroy your right to organize, vote, speak freely, write freely..."

I paused, recalling that I get subsidies for writing and producing my musical docudramas emphasizing multicultural education and it seemed that I benefited from everything politics and politicians offered because of their kindness and concern for this country. Immediately, my attitude turned to gratitude.

"But, Dee, I'm shocked that politics could be involved in the Simpson trial."

"Life's getting so complicated, Alice, maybe we all should have a passionate commitment to religion in order to maintain our sanity in this political world where the bottom line is always 'The Almighty's dollar."

"Well I've got news for you, Dee. Even doctors are concerned about patients who have a passionate commitment to religion and have found that it is excellent mind/body medicine. They tell me we're getting a lot of medical converts who're now reading the Bible. Can you imagine medical doctors reading the Bible?"

"They ought to; people's lives are in their hands."

I smiled. "And they're helping people with God's hands."

"And you're helping your husband with God's hands, feet, mind, body."

"And we're using God's mind, body and money when we help each other."

"All right, I get the picture. We're one in the spirit."

"Anyway, Dee, the Bible's interesting reading! I fell in love with it because of the Simpson trial," I said into the noise of energetic children enjoying their colorful playground with its large playhouse, Angel Fish Rocker, Ruff 'n Tumble Ball Pit, Tropical Play Slide, Wave Climber, Junior Activity Gym and all the play equipment that politics bought. The children's joy made us want to be children again.

I thought about an article in the January 20 issue of *Newsweek* magazine entitled "The Strange World of JonBenet," the little six-year-old beauty queen who was fatally abused. I thought about the mutilated body of four-year-old Kendia Lockheart here in Miami whose father was once arrested for child abuse and aggravated battery against his two-year old daughter. I thought about the thousands of little children and women who are abused daily as tears rolled down my cheeks and I wiped them away with the back of my hand. I thought about the hate mail Black students have recently found in their lockers that read "I hate all niggers," and how the caring Dade County School Board is looking seriously into this crime.

Dee stared at me wide eyed. "I had no idea Simpson's trials touched you like that. I suppose his trial has saved a lot of souls, lives and marriages. Do you plan to further research the Old and New Testament?"

"Yes, but right now I'm still researching *Genesis* and looking into science and original sin," I answered, enjoying the healthy laughter of innocent tots.

"And you're gonna write about it to save the world. Lord, help you!"

"No, I'm gonna write about it to save Alice's world," I said, feeling grateful that she made me aware of the politics surrounding the Trial of the Century. This awakening could be the answer to questions about the spiritual message of the case that were disturbing to me. I needed to focus in on domestic violence.

Could it be that a friend is really the masterpiece of nature?

2
"Speak, Lord, thy servant is listening."
1 Samuel 3:9

Dee and I said our goodbyes and I was enroute home when the Creator's messages from the Simpson case flashed before me like a neon light. The brutality of American Slavery and the Holocaust were the highest forms of racism and domestic violence we children of the universe could ever thrust upon each other. There were valuable, spiritual lessons to be learned from these evils, yet these evils did not get one-ninetieth the attention the Simpson case was getting. It is indeed my firm belief that many of us were obsessed with the Simpson case because it was the will of the Creator that we listen. It was not our will because there were many times when I wanted to tune out any mention of the case but for some powerful reason, I felt drawn to listen and learn.

We blamed the media for sensationalizing the trials but deep within my heart I felt it was the universe bringing us a universal message. And the agony of trying to find this full message pierced and is yet piercing my heart. It bothers me that our churches are much too quiet about the revelations.

Politics! Yes, politics...just as the brutalities of American Slavery and the Holocaust were rooted in politics. In politics, the bottom line is always the almighty dollar.

It was Black History Month and many children across the nation were learning about slavery and its spiritual message. I recalled contents of a speech delivered by a White slave owner, William Lynch, in 1712 on the bank of the James River in the colony of Virginia. The speech was given following a Negro slave revolt that occurred in New York City after which many slaves were slaughtered, lynched or burned at the stake. When I arrived home, I hurriedly pulled the document from the files and read it, feeling heavyhearted. My girlfriend, Vennie Huff, from Cincinnati, Ohio had sent me the material for further research from the University of Cincinnati Department of African-American Studies.

The document entitled, *Let's Make A Slave*, compiled by the Black Archives Liberation Library in 1970 is the study of the scientific process of man-breaking and slave making. It describes the "rationale and results of the Anglo Saxon's ideas and methods of insuring the master/slave relationship."

According to the study, the letter is called *The Willie Lynch Speech*, and was used religiously by the institution of slavery. Mr. Lynch, in his letter, stated that he had a fool proof method (a kit) of controlling Black slaves that would keep Blacks enslaved for at least 300 years or more for good economic reasons. He outlined a number of human differences among the Blacks, and took the differences and made them bigger. He stated that he used fear, distrust and envy for control purposes, and assured the White slaveholders that distrust is stronger than adulation, respect or admiration. He stated that on top of his "list is 'age,' the second is 'color,' there is intelligence, hair (fine or coarse), height, size, sex," etc., in order to divide and conquer.

Mr. Lynch taught slaveholders how to pitch one Black against the other, creating distrust such as: young Black males versus Old Black males; light skinned Blacks versus dark-skinned Blacks; female Blacks versus male Blacks, etc. He stated in the letter how slaveholders must (psychologically) break Blacks from one form of human life to another..i.e., keep the body and take the mind, annihilate the (African) mother tongue and institute the English language that involves the new life's work, but never teach slaves how to read English...the language of the slaveholder. He urged slaveholders to kill the protective Black male image, etc.

William Lynch implied that if the slaveholder breaks the spirit and mental strength of the Black mother, she will break the offspring in its early years of development and when the offspring is old enough to work, "she will deliver it up to you for her normal female protective tendencies will have been lost in the original breaking process." He further informed the slaveholders that: "You must have your White servants and overseers distrust all Blacks, but it is necessary that slaves trust and depend on us. They must love, respect and trust only us."

In closing, Mr. Lynch said: "Gentlemen, these kits are your keys to control. Use them. Have your wives and children use them, never miss an opportunity. If used intensely for one year, the Blacks themselves will remain perpetually distrustful." He stated that "the Black slave, after receiving this indoctrination, shall carry on and will become self refueling and self-generating for hundreds of years, maybe thousands."

The reports spoke of involuntary servitude when slaves were considered chattel. White politicians taught the masses that Blacks were not human beings, and Whites were religiously taught to believe this evil and vicious untruth from the depths of their hearts. The Euro-American slave trade continued from the 1500s to the 1800s. The most reliable estimate range from ten million to twenty million Blacks. On the eve of the Civil War, there were four million Black slaves in the South.

Listening to my heart, I sadly thought about man's inhumanity to man and the spiritual lessons learned from this violent experience. I thought about the similar experience of our present day political climate concerning the unborn fetus and the Partial-Birth Abortion Ban Act which I along with millions of concerned citizens and churches are spiritually supporting so that children will not be brutally killed only seconds before they are born.

My attitude was gratitude when I thought about the power of spirituality and how its principles awakened political slaveholders and brought an end to American slavery and its brutality. Then, tearfully praying, I whispered to the universe: Perhaps spirituality could do the same for the unborn child who is considered not a human being by most of our well-meaning political leaders. Perhaps they, too, will listen to their hearts because the heart reveals love's truest feelings, especially in words of the song, "*America, The Beautiful*", written by Katherine L. Bates:

America! America! God mend thine every flaw
Confirm thy soul in self control...Thy liberty in law.

Based on the theory, "Trust Life and It Will Teach You," love's truest feelings were miraculously exemplified when more than 130 million viewers watched the *Roots mini-series*. It became the most successful mini-series in television history, sweeping the Nineteenth Annual Emmy Award presentations in Los Angeles, California winning 36 unprecedented nominations. The *Roots mini-series*, based on Alex Haley's novel of the same title in which Haley traced his ancestry to Africa and American slavery, ended eight nights of superb presentations on the ABC television network. It has been officially reported that the Sunday night final achieved the highest single ratings ever amassed by a television production. The previous top television presentation had been the epic Civil War drama, *Gone With The Wind*, by Margaret Mitchell.

Even O.J. Simpson had a split-second character role in the *Roots mini-series* in which Haley showed that some of our own, greedy African ancestors had a hand in selling us Blacks into slavery but unaware that we would be treated as being inhuman.

After reading the document I thought to myself, "Distrust is stronger than adulation, respect or admiration when one wants to create hate, divide and destroy a people." American slavery was the epitome of domestic violence here on planet earth because of its physical cruelty and the psychological effects of the slave system.

Yes, it was February, 1997, Black History month and the children were learning about Black history, charting our evolving paths from the savagery of slavery to the present day before O.J.'s fall. We, as a united nation, had courageously come a long way from slavery to the present day in which Blacks like O.J. (before the fall) could rise to their highest potentials in a democratic society and be respected and loved by all humanity. We, as united Americans, enjoyed applauding our spiritual progress as children of the universe in which our multiculturalness is a gift. Only in a democracy can this miracle happen. That is why when we sing *America the Beautiful*, we cannot help but shed tears of love and joy. Especially in the Bates verse that reads: "*O beautiful for patriot dream that sees beyond the years,...Thine alabaster cities gleam undimmed by human tears,...America! America! God shed his grace on thee...And crown thy good with brotherhood from sea to shining sea.*"

In brotherhood, we were beautifully moving forward. And suddenly the O.J. Simpson tragedy exploded into the calm and the strife, thundering messages into our multicultural society and creating the great divide. The reason why history keeps repeating itself is because many of us keep sweeping its spiritual lessons under the rug.

So why is the Simpson Case...a case that mesmerized the media and public... getting such world-wide attention and being called the cultural mania of the century with its "vicious murders, trail of blood, wealthy celebrity defendant, star attorneys, biracial marriage, sensational police chase, flurry of media coverage, tales of drug and sexual escapades, reports of spousal abuse and charges of racism?" Because, according to both my good friends, Dee and Sally, it's a wake-up call for us as multicultural children of the universe to stop the violence throughout the world, racial and domestic, and let us continue the spiritual journey as we help each other evolve as children of Planet Earth. The case has changed forever the way we look at race, sex, celebrityhood, lawyers, juries, police, soap operas and moral and spiritual values. The spiritual message extends far beyond Mr. Simpson's life and tragedy. Actually, the spiritual message is beyond human comprehension.

(Note: Although results of the Simpson cases were not being given credit for the courageous moves made by major religious denominations confessing to the sin of racism, I feel without a doubt that this is the Creator's work. "He that has ears, let him hear." Those leaders who heard the higher calling and bravely responded are, indeed, a cut above human. They are in the category with saints. As mentioned earlier the denominations were the 15.6 million-member Southern Baptist Convention in June 20,1995, and the four major religious denominations in South Carolina: Lutheran, Anglican, Roman Catholic and United Methodist churches that represent more than 450,000 members, May 16, 1997).

When John Newton, a White man born in 1779 who exported over several hundred-thousand Blacks to be sold into brutal American slavery, awakened from this sin of man's inhumanity to man and wrote the powerful song, *Amazing Grace How Sweet the Sound*, his awakening lifted him to a cut above human. So powerful is that hymn that it is sung in perhaps every religious denomination throughout this nation! Whenever we feel that amazing grace from the depths of our hearts, it brings us to our knees with tears of joy!

Amazing grace, how sweet the sound
That saved a wretch like me!
I once was lost, but now I'm found,
Was blind, but now I see.
'Twas grace that taught my heart to fear,
And grace my fears relieved;
How precious did that grace appear,
The hour I first believed!

In his bestseller, *The Celestine Prophecy*, James Redfield portrays human beings as experiencing life through a new spiritual "common sense," and that people of this nature are mysteriously drawn to each other. Based on this theory, I can understand the courageous move of John Newton and those brave religious denominational leaders who confessed to the sin of slavery and racism and asked forgiveness. Indeed, they have been called to lead the way in experiencing life through this new spiritual "common sense." It would be miraculous if we would all follow their pursuit to let the healing begin.

It was my conversation with Dee that helped me awaken to the spiritual message of the Simpson trials. I now understand why she is one of my best friends with whom I enjoy communicating; we both are experiencing life through this new spiritual "common sense." I also understand why my husband, through enlightenment, had grasped the spiritual message of the Simpson trials ever since the beginning of the case, and how he finally drew me into his perception to the point where my life's spiritual journey has amazingly become a living example of Redfield's prophecy. I am awed at the various levels of spiritual growth we encounter enroute, and the wonderful personalities awaiting us at each growth station that lead us to the next.

In like manner, I've always been awed by how the universe used multiple sclerosis to help John and me experience life through a new spiritual "common sense." And now I m awed by how it is using the Simpson trials to bring all of us children of the universe into this broader perception to let the healing begin. In *The Celestine Prophecy*, Redfield implied that experiencing life is a mystery to be lived as we journey toward a completely spiritual culture here on Planet Earth where we humans are a gift to one another.

Yes, communicating with my friend, Dee, made me aware of the trials message and that friends are, indeed, the masterpiece of nature.

(**Note:** Four months later, and after this manuscript was completed, Dee shared with me her insight on the national apology for slavery made on June 14, 1997, by President Clinton ten days prior to the third anniversary of the Simpson tragedy. She said that I should feel grateful that America always tries to do the right thing; and that the apology was not from Whitefolks to Blackfolks, but from Congress, on behalf of America, to the descendants of Black slaves, we African Americans. Apologizing was the right thing to do because America supported the importation of millions of unoffending Africans and has never officially expressed its apology...i.e., its apology for putting millions of Blacks in bondage and reducing them to livestock. Dee implied that American slavery did not rise by accident; slavery was dirty politics, and most of the woes of African Americans today started with slavery. As an educator who knows that the past touches the present and shapes the future, she feels that without slavery and the racism that made it possible, there would be no huge gaps in academic achievement, no unequal opportunities, no high crime rate, and no disproportionate poverty. She said that America bears complicity in the pain of its African-American children. Dee commented that when we consider the national and international respect, love and appreciation given African Americans like talk show hostess Oprah Winfrey for her exceptional talent and a few others, we can see that America is spiritually evolving and trying to do the right thing in spite of politics).

Anyway, back to the present date, Monday, February 3, I was beginning to experience feelings of extreme frustrations and anger. Why? Because Simpson who, too, was once respected, loved and appreciated by all nationalities in spite of politics, was a wife abuser; and Dee's insight on politics provided me the political implications of domestic violence and its false sense of security.

CHAPTER FIVE

To start with the self and try to understand all things is delusion. To let the self be awakened by all things is enlightenment. -Kigen Dogen

Friends are special. After walking with Dee and being awakened to the truth that politics and politicians control our outer life, I was ready to stop being overly concerned about the trials because politics seemed to be the main focus while two people remained incarcerated.

In my world, domestic abuse was a main issue, and it seemed that, because of blindness, we were about to push it again on the back burner.

Following my walk with Dee, I visited my husband and took him on a short educational and enjoyable sightseeing tour via Metrorail. And now I was back in my home-based office eagerly researching material I had gathered on domestic violence because I was beginning to see its evil destruction. The Trial of the Century had revealed to me that domestic violence and abuse shatters the continuity of the family, it destroys healthy relationships, it destroys individuals and it destroys spirituality.

But I was still writing around a writer's block which I now considered to be abusive. I kept focusing on the known truth that writing is our mind/body medicine that keeps our spirits alive; especially while the jury was still deliberating as to whether or not Simpson would be held liable for the double murders. He had won custody of his two young children and was ecstatically grateful.

Many of us African Americans were happy too but I, being a former victim of wife abuse, felt somewhat uncomfortable.

This evening, my mind was determined to dominate my decisions with episodes of profiles in gratitude, because gratitude is the basis of human happiness and it blocks all forms of depression and makes one humble. I felt grateful for the enthusiasm to write again on the subject of domestic abuse and not be distracted by blind prejudices.

At one time I was was deeply concerned that Ms. Rosemary Carraway, the lone Black juror for the civil trial, was dismissed because her daughter worked for the Los Angeles district attorney's office, but I tried to ignore my frustrations and stay focused on domestic violence.

Recalling a wise statement from my creative writing professor and other writers that one cannot write when he's forever in the street, and that one needs to stay focused, I had hurriedly completed the late evening one-mile walk, talking to the universe and expressing my gratitude, and then had rushed home, anxious to communicate with the computer and stay focused on the battered wife. In the research, I would highlight some common characteristics of male batterers, and and also pinpoint domestic violence effects on children.

Searching the beige lateral files, I pulled one of the folders of documented materials I had been compiling since the beginning of the trial.

One report from the files stated that every fifteen seconds a woman is battered in the United States by her husband, boyfriend, or live-in partner. Another report stated that domestic violence is the leading cause of injury to women between ages 15 to 44, more common than automobile accidents, muggings and cancer deaths combined.

When I read that half of all women will experience some form of violence from their partners during marriage, and that more than one-third are battered repeatedly every year, I knew I needed to join the women fighting this universal battle.

"What these statistics do reveal about domestic violence is alarming," I said to the universe, reading silently and learning that there are at least four million reported incidents of domestic violence against women every year. Reading further, I found that women are six times more likely than men to be victims of violent crimes in intimate relationships; that weapons are used in thirty percent of domestic violence incidents; that fifteen to twenty-five percent of pregnant women are battered; and that in ninety-five percent of all domestic violence assaults, crimes are committed by men against women.

Reading further, I learned that as violence against women becomes more severe and more frequent in the home, children experience a three-hundred percent increase in physical violence by the male batterer. To learn that approximately one out of every twenty-five elderly persons is victimized annually, was frightening. I thought about my unfinished manuscript, *Kennetta*, when I read that more than fifty-three percent of male abusers beat their children, and wondered should I reveal that Kennetta had to serve prison time for defending her life against her abusive father.

Why don't battered wives leave? I was anxious to answer that question because I had lived it with my ex-husband and so had my playmother, Patty. I also knew that women who leave their abusive husbands are at a greater risk of being killed by the husband than those who stay because that's why Patty was killed. Writing on this subject was painful; and again my fingers moved hesitantly into the flow of thoughts that encircled a world of experiences waiting for some occult Power, as usual to move my mind, sharing its wisdom into problems of today's living. *Genesis* and domestic violence, I thought to myself, meditating, researching and typing late into the night.

The following morning was Tuesday, February 4, and the civil jury was still deliberating. Keeping my mind focused on what Dee's implication that the entire case had nothing to do with justice but was tainted with politics, and that the bottom line was 'The Almighty' dollar, I exhaled.

And now, feeling as though I was being guided by some directing agency, I began typing on the psychological foundations of domestic abuse which I had been researching. Much of the material came from my own experiences and blended in with my nineteen years in psychotherapy.

Hours later, the telephone jingled. It was John's social worker from the VA Medical Center reminding me of the eleven o'clock Interdisciplinary meeting to evaluate my husband's medical progress. I was baffled that this all important meeting had slipped my memory, and felt angry with my unconscious obsession with my "Waiting for the verdict" stress disorder for stealing the focus from my husband's illness.

Glancing at my watch, I noticed it was already ten o'clock.

"What?" I shrieked and shut down the computer; then realized that I did not save the new material on the psychological foundations of DV added to the disk.

"Oh no-o-o-o!" I groaned with clinched fist, my arms raised in a boxer's pose. "How could you?"

"How could you not?" replied my higher consciousness. "Your mind is being tortured that the jury's decision, regardless of whether it's a guilty on not guilty verdict is going to increase racial tensions in the country."

I understood, and decided to leave my "mounting depression" in denial because it was too uncomfortable to deal with at this time. And I didn't want to handle it anyway. I wanted to back away from any thoughts of the trial as the analyst had suggested before my frustrated attitude took control, blocking my ability to reason objectively.

After hurriedly dressing and feeling angry with my mind for forgetting the meeting and forgetting to save the new material, I jumped into John's Chrysler handicap van and weaved through heavy traffic, rushing to the nursing home to be with my husband as we both listened to his fate.

Enroute, and needing help for troubled, overloaded thoughts and feelings, I entered a counseling session with the universe, believing in the entire spiritual energy of the mind that brings peace.

The atmosphere of the conference room was peaceful and relaxing as each member of the various caregiving disciplines gave well-organized medical reports on John's activities, participation and progress.

How could anyone accept the knowledge that John was once very abusive. I felt grateful that the analyst had stopped the violence that was triggered by MS, and had helped our marriage to successfully survive.

My mind felt calm. I sat quietly, squeezing John's hand and letting my thoughts computerize the strategies of how love was being expressed through kindness and concern by a nursing staff of caregivers.

John's private sitter, Mrs. Baker, had brought him to the conference and, every so often, was asked her observation on his responses to various medical and rehab treatments. She was very sophisticated in responding.

Listening attentively, I took notes as the doctors and nurses spoke with seriousness and concern, relieved that my husband's blood pressure was again normal, that his month-long out-of-control blood sugar was now under control, his weight was now normal after shaving off a few calories from his daily menu. The trigeminal neuralgia was under control. The nurse reported she was using Capsaicin, a topical analgesic cream on the left side of John's face that was recommended by the doctor. This cream was used in lieu of tegretol and seemed to be far more effective.

Smiling, I turned to my husband and whispered: "So, that's why you set my lips on fire everytime I kissed your handsome golden face?"

He chuckled. "Oh boy."

I listened as the medical staff continued their reports and recalled the many years John and I had wrestled with his trigeminal neuralgia that kept his jaw in excruciating pain for days. We were so grateful to VA for professional services.

"The bedsore is definitely healing," said a medium-built, Caucasian nurse, her curly hair cut neatly in a bob. "We measured it yesterday and it's getting smaller. "

At this I wanted to shout my "Thank You's" to the universe and do the Electric Slide, the Macarena, and the Tongoneo all over the conference room and down the hallway. What a blessing, I thought to myself. You angels are helping other angels with God's hands.

The nurse continued: "Although Dr. Johnson is basically confined to bed, we take him out of bed every other day for at least two hours. Within those two hours, his private sitter, Mrs. Baker, often takes him outside for fresh air and sunshine. He seems to enjoy the new schedule. Later, we'll allow him to stay up a little longer as the bedsore continues to heal. You see, Mrs. Johnson, we don't want to put too much pressure on the wound while it's slowly healing."

I understood their concern. That was why John and I took a very short tour on yesterday. Once before when he resumed activities while the bedsore was healing, the ulcer flared up again because of too much pressure that was being placed on it, even though John was in an air-cushioned chair designed to combat pressure. He had to, again, be confined to bed. This experience had taught the hospital medical staff to take no chances.

Following the conference, I thanked the staff for the outstanding nursing care given my husband and for continued kindness and concern. John thanked the medical staff too, smiling and nodding his head.

It was lunchtime when he returned to his room. The sitter dressed him for bed and later, I hand-fed him the balanced diet prepared by skillful dietitians who knew the art of preparing healthy food to keep my husband's diabetes, high blood pressure and history of urinary tract infections under good control.

"Let's talk about our gratitude to the nursing team for excellent caregiving?" I suggested, removing the food tray and anxious to pick his brains to discover what further wisdom about life experiences his solitude had taught him.

Actually, I wanted to talk about *Genesis* in relation to today's society because I was beginning to see it continuously being re-lived. As a Morehouse graduate, John was more sophisticated than I about the books of the Bible. He flunked the course in Religion because he was one of the thousands of voices questioning some of the human behavior portrayed in *Genesis* by people who were supposed to be seen as heroes, but he always managed to believe that love is the essence of life. And now, at the end of three million years, religious leaders are beginning to ponder the same questions these inquiring minds were asking. After all, it was Stephen Hawkings the renown scientist with Lou Gehrig's disease, who said that the universe is out here waiting to be understood, and that includes the Holy Bible.

Following my intuition, I decided to work the subject into our discussions of medical report findings, and to cautiously mention the O. J. Simpson civil trial and our obsession with it because of its educational proponents. I shared with him some of the information I learned from Atty. Cochran's book, *Journey To Justice*, that spoke of his life spent in the legal system as an advocate for the law and for the individual. I told John that I especially appreciated Mr. Cochran's statement that each time the courtroom is brought to order, we're all on trial. That's the way I perceived the Simpson case, and that's why I was so locked into it. We listen and learn.

I also shared with him a quick review of Mr. Darden's bestseller, *In Contempt*, telling John the book is a masterpiece in which Mr. Darden gave his own impressions of the case, and that I hoped the jury hadn't read the book before making their own decisions. "Both books are powerfully written and very educational," I said, now thumbing through the pages. "I'm sure they'll be required reading in the schools, colleges and universities."

We talked about the courageous lawyers and I read to him some of seeds of doubts stated in Mr. Cochran's book, pausing as he made comments.

"Oh boy," he said, admitting that we are being educated.

"President Clinton's State of the Union speech is going to be tonight, John. I'll stay with you until six, then I'm heading home to hear the speech. If the verdict comes in during that time, there's gonna be a big struggle for TV dominance!"

"You can hear it here with me."

"No way; I want to use my remote control freely!" I fluffed his pillow and replaced it under his head. "Your medical report was quite impressive, baby."

He nodded. "Yes-s-s-s! The nursing team's very kind."

"Oftentimes we fail to see this."

"Because... oftentimes... we fail to be grateful, Alice."

"Well, thanks for your keen observation. It seems the Simpson case is helping me to study the Bible and learn a brand new lesson in the joys of gratitude."

"The Simpson trial was educational but I wasn't talking about you. I was talking about people in general."

"Even so, I feel guilty of the crime of not being grateful. I've formed the habit of taking a close look at my own behavior to learn from my mistakes. One's self is an excellent teacher. It projects a lot of selfishness."

"Other people are excellent teachers, too."

"Yes, especially those interesting guys in *Genesis*. Their behaviors reveal to us that we're designed by natural selection to conceal selfish motives from ourselves. We've a natural blindness to our nature and it makes life a little difficult for us to show our kindness and concern for other people. But, this has to do with one's own thoughts and feelings, John."

He smiled. "I know. And I meant.... other people's... thoughts and feelings can... be excellent teachers, Alice. And...especially in *Genesis*."

I agreed and thought about lessons in courage and love the case had taught me..in most instances scripture-based faith.

"What did you learn from the case, so far?" I asked, knowing I was not using my therapy as counseled. It's difficult to ignore Shakespeare's dramas.

"Wisdom."

"Do you think some people are born with the wisdom of love?"

"Jesus Christ was."

"I mean other people."

He nodded his head. "Most religious...ministers...are."

"And that's why they're called to spread the message of love."

Again, he nodded his head, then scratched his neck.

"Well, according to your theory, women who know the wisdom of love can be called to spread the message, too."

He smiled. "Do you... want to be... one?"

I gaped. "No way! I had no reference to myself. But if we want to help stop the violence, we women need to start preaching love. It seems you men who commit all this violence aren't doing such a good job of stopping the abuse."

"The men in the Bible didn't either."

"Except Jesus. I guess we all have a ministry. Mine is being a caregiver. I had reference to a woman being a priest, a rabbi, a preacher of the Gospel. Why didn't Jesus have a woman disciple?"

"Ask the universe."

I grinned, then pulled up a chair and sat by his bedside to carefully trim his fingernails. "Ever since the Simpson trials, the universe and I have become the best of friends inasmuch as you're here at the nursing home and I'm often alone. I love her theory which implies that we should be more grateful. It's the same as Father Clancy's philosophy of 'Let your attitude be gratitude!'"

"Maybe...someone's putting in..a good..word..for..us all."

"I'm sure someone is because every time I talk with the universe, it still responds basically with: "Since love is the only answer, what then is the question?"

"Good!."

"And because of this, I'm beginning to take a closer look at the experiences in my life and highlight how often folks have shown kindness and concern toward other folks, and thank my Creator for this show of love. Seeing this, I'm gonna begin expressing gratitude that we're all evolving slowly into being human in spite of all the horrible behavior we hear about through the media, and all the different kinds of illnesses that plague our lives. In every relationship with each other, we teach either love or hate. We women want to teach love, wisdom! The wisdom of love! But where is wisdom born, in experiences?"

"In suffering," John replied, then began talking about the many sermons of Martin Luther King that often spoke on the subject.

"I'm still wondering why do good folks suffer?"

"No cross, no crown."

"Sounds like my mother who used to sing: 'The consecrated cross I'll bear.' When I was a child I though the words were: 'the constipated cross-eyed bear.' That was as funny as the kid who used to sing "God bless America...stand beside her and guide her through the night with a light from a bulb' ..b-u-l-b."

John chuckled, "'When I was a child, I thought as a child.'"

"'I acted and understood as a child, but when I became a woman I put away all childish things.' But aren't we taught that we are to be as innocent little children in order to meet the God that's within us?"

When I was about to add that sickness and death are great teachers, Nurse DuVal entered the room to turn my husband as scheduled. She said he needed to rest on his right side. I wanted to thank her for interrupting my conversation because I felt myself getting too preoccupied with wisdom born in suffering. But then

I thought about the Biblical character Job and wondered does the wisdom come first and is ignored, then the individual's suffering snaps us to attention? Perhaps we are too preoccupied with earning a living to listen to the life's teachings that have been handed down through the ages.

"But, haven't we been religiously reading the Holy Bible...especially *Genesis* to gain wisdom?" I asked the universe, excusing myself from the area as Nurse DuVal pulled the curtain to respect John's privacy while she attended him.

I stood outside John's bedroom door and continued talking with the universe about the art of forgiving one another. "*Forgiveness takes away what stands between your brother and yourself*," I recalled reading in Marianne Williamson's book *A Return to Love*.

Life experiences had taught us that the key to inner peace is forgiveness because our thoughts and feelings are transformed from fear to love. When we are able to see the wounds in other people, and see other people as ourselves, we are able to forgive. And this forgiveness is expressed through kindness and concern.

This was exemplified in the book of *Genesis*...in Joseph's abandonment by his brothers. And then the forgiveness that healed family wounds. A forgiveness that was expressed through kindness and concern.

"Perhaps you humans should return to your spiritual roots, and the Bible is the ultimate source if you're a follower of the teachings of Jesus," said the universe. "Abraham is your founding father."

Again I though about an incident that happened in the 1960s during the time we were peacefully demonstrating for our equal rights and getting killed by White policemen and other racists for doing so. Some of us Christians wondered why did God allow some people to be so hateful toward others and to deny others their civil rights. Having a childhood understanding of the Creator, I searched the Holy Bible for an adult understanding about racial hatred. I recalled telling my university professor about my search and he blatantly said that the Bible is a series of fairy tales. But he failed to say that they were based on moral and spiritual teachings. I recalled how painful this message was and how I, upon arriving home from class, felt hopeless and lost, and feared that I would feel that way for the rest of my life. Throughout the long and dreary night, I twisted and turned in bed, praying that the statements the professor made were untruths, and pleading for understanding and a return to my former state of security. After hours of sobbing and feeling heartbroken, I fell asleep and entered into a series of terrifying dreams in which I was smothering in a large, empty room filled with heavy clouds of black smoke. In the dream, I was fighting desperately to move through this huge mountain of blinding smoke, stumbling and falling, coughing, choking, and pleading for help. Suddenly when I said "Lord, have mercy," I immediately awoke, stared into the darkness of night, then fell to my knees in prayer, my heart pounding heavily within me. Hours later, breathing quietly, and still on bended knees, I vowed to ignore the professor's comments and cling to my childhood faith that "God is love" and love is all that matters.. just as my parents had taught me before I could even talk. Mothers have gotta teach their infants the wisdom of love, I pleaded with the universe.

And now as I stood in the hallway of VA Nursing Home -2 awaiting Nurse DuVal's call that she had finished attending my husband, I felt good that my meditation was enabling me to understand more clearly the Book of *Genesis* and its moral themes that indeed, preoccupy today's society, thanks to the Trial of the Century, and Oprah's talks on self-esteem.

"*Genesis* is merely showing us that the love of our neighbor is the essential action of human existence, and the only way in which we can actually experience God," I whispered. "John's illness has taught me that God can reach us only through the medium of the love of our neighbor. I had to love my husband, even while he was abusive, in order to reach the God inside me."

Nurse DuVal's "Okay now" sounded into my reflections.

"You may come back in now, Mrs. Johnson," she said softly, hurrying from the room.

I rushed in, almost bumping into her.

So anxious was I to talk with John about my new understanding, I forgot to express gratitude to the nurse for turning my husband. And because I took seriously what was learned from the TV trial implications that we so-called Christians often overlook deeds of our neighbors who express love through kindness and concern, and that we should program our minds to be Christlike, I ran from the room to find the nurse; scurrying up and down the hallway, pivoting from room to room in my search to locate her. Where had she gone so quickly?

"Who're you looking for, Mrs. Johnson?" asked Mrs. Lopez, the nursing assistant, her Jamaican accent stanched and clear.

"Nurse DuVal. " I wanted to forget the trial and focus on people.

Pausing as she adjusted another patient more comfortably in his wheel chair, Mrs. Lopez said, "Nurse DuVal had to rush back to continue taking care of another patient who's having problems breathing 'cause he has pneumonia, Mrs. Johnson. She only left the patient in order to turn Mr. Johnson 'cause it was time for him to be turned."

And now I really was pained because, in my own selfish anxiety to tell John about *Genesis* which explains why we are what we are... (and which sounded more like juicy gossip than anything else), I forgot to thank the kind nurse for turning my husband. When I explained this to Mrs. Lopez she laughed and said, "Don't worry about it, Mrs. Johnson. As nurses, we just do our duties and thank the Good Lord for strength and love to do them, child." I had to do my gratitude assignment.

The beauty inside her was shining through. I smiled into her neighborly smile, thanked her, and continued down the hallway until I found Nurse DuVal and thanked her.

"Oh, Mrs. Johnson, it wasn't necessary for you to rush down

here just to thank me," she smiled and said, adjusting the oxygen mask of the disabled elderly patient. "We nurses do what we have to do."

"Instinctively, hum?"

"It seems that way, Mrs. Johnson."

"Amazing! We do things by instinct and by intuition."

"Instinct is natural intuition power."

"I'm beginning to understand that now. It's been said that if we wish to see love in action, visit the hospitals."

Again she smiled and, without pausing from her work, said gently: "Well, that's a nice way to look at it. Sick people need help, Mrs. Johnson. I wanted to be a nurse so that I could help. I'm pretty sure most nurses come to the profession with that attitude."

I watched as she made notes on the bed chart. "Nursing's undoubtedly your mission because you seem so comfortable doing it."

"It's challenging. I used to be a research analyst at the University of Miami prior to becoming a registered nurse."

"Blessed is the nurse who has found her work," I said as we both left the room, recalling how blessed O.J. was for finding his work as a great athlete.

"Oh, with a master's degree in science, I enjoyed being a research analyst..dealing with loads of interesting data. But, I also wanted to work in a similar profession that would also provide interpersonal relationships."

She doesn't care for a lot of solitude because she knows how to balance her life, I thought to myself. Having learned from my life experiences with MS that interpersonal relationship and personal interests are the major sources of human happiness, and that all human beings need interest as well as relationships, I said: "Being a nurse calls for lots and lots of patience with sick patients."

"I enjoy the patients," she said enroute to the nursing station, pausing to help a handicap veteran who was struggling to move his wheelchair from the path of others in wheelchairs going in opposite directions.

"Blessed are VA patients who have a patient nurse like Nurse DuVal," I said, re-entering John's room and almost bumping head-on into Mrs. Lopez and her armload of bed linens.

Seeing this, John chuckled and said, " Blessed are.. your eyes... for not getting ..bashed in... with Mrs. Lopez's.. fist."

"Then she'd be a batterer." I jiggled his ear and he laughed.

"Guess what, John?" I said, suggesting that he put his laughter on hold. "The universe and and I had a good conversation about the book of *Genesis*. You know what? *Genesis* has drawn a new surge of interest in the past few months, and I recall that my university professor and I had a serious disagreement about that book. He called it a cult. But, John, the book speaks to our modern society and tells us why we are what we are. And it..."

He interrupted. "Don't you know... who you are... by now?"

I marched about the room, massaging my hands and searching for a captivating response. "Yes, John. I'm a child of this great, big universe...an extension of God's love."

"...To love... the universe... and other... people, Alice," he added.

"Correct. And we children of the universe spend our lives learning how."

"Good!"

"I recalled my analyst saying years ago when I used to have trouble dealing with you and your MS and abusiveness and with other people on my church committee that man's a social being who needs the companionship and the affection of other human beings from cradle to grave. Religious cults don't teach that."

"I'm glad he awakened... you to... that."

"So am I, sweetheart. But, actually, battling with your mysterious illness taught me that interpersonal relationships of an intimate kind are the chief source of happiness. So, I continued being in love with you because it held the key to my own happiness.

You might call it selfish but I call it survival, honey, because you were a trip!"

"Oh boy!" He kneaded his forehead, laughing. "My uncles were abusive."

I laughed too. "One of your uncles used to take his sawed-off shotgun and beat the stew outta his common-law wife. One day he cracked her across the head so hard, Grandma had to kick his butt. When he got sick and was paralyzed with a stroke because of diabetes and high blood pressure she left his evil disabled behind in that hospital bed and ran away. She ran away because even from his hospital bed, he was verbally abusing her. I hope she's not a bag lady after being abused throughout that common-law marriage."

He looked at me teary eyed. "Are you gonna leave me?"

"No way! You're nothing like him! You've become an enlightened angel. Your parents taught you about love and our White analyst...as Neil used to call him... taught us how to deal with our problems. You and I used our therapy, fell in love again with each other and began living a productive life, turning MS into a blessing to help us write our thoughts and feelings. And now we write musical docudramas emphasizing multicultural education to help promote social justice, universal peace and brotherly love! You know, we'll be in production this Friday!"

He smiled and said humorously, "Oh boy. The White, White Whity White analyst did a good job!"

"With his counseling, we let the healing begin!"

"Write that down and thank him."

"I'm wrestling with writer's block."

"No-way."

"That's what I told O.J. My being overly tenseful about his trials almost drove me nuts! I had to back-off! The analyst suggested I stop prejudging. He wanted me to look at it as an educational tool. It was difficult to be color blind, and still is. But, I'm hanging in here with my writer's block blocking everything

I attempt to write. I'm hurt about the victims. I can't even think!"

"People never stop thinking, Alice."

"Then, I'll continue to write all the confusion I'm thinking because I see the 'little child' in everyone. If I don't write, I'll probably end up like the bag lady."

He rolled his eyes at me and shook his head. "Write!"

"Okay!" I said with outstretched palms. Then pausing, I laughed and continued: "The mind is always thinking, I'm gonna write about my writer's block. Maybe that's what the universe wants me to do anyway. "

"Write, Alice. Use your therapy."

"'And use your therapy to write all the racial anger out of your system' as Dr. Kensinger would probably say," I added, then took the container of Nature Shower Hand and Body Lotion from the nightstand and began massaging his dry-looking hands and face as we continued laughing and talking.

"Actually, John sweetheart, in struggling to work with you and your MS, and watching that drama unfold on TV, I've learned that there's no happiness in getting, only in giving."

He pushed my hand from his face. "Well... don't be giving... my eyes a massage... with all that... lotion, Alice! That's enough!"

"I'm sorry. My mind was locked into those turbulent days you and I spent trying to cope with MS."

"That's ..in the past."

"I know that's in the past, John. But, I was thinking about the lessons we learned and are still learning through solitude. Someone said conversation enriches the understanding, but solitude is the school of genius."

"And... too much of it can... make you... nutty."

"Well, with you in this nursing home, I thought I was going nutty being at home alone and in solitude until I started watching the TV case and talking with the universe."

"And what did... the universe... have to say?"

"The universe said that some of the world's greatest thinkers lived in solitude. They never got married, never raised a family, most of them lived alone...in solitude. Men of genius like Jesus, ...Spinoza..."

"Descartes.."

"Locke, Newton, Kant. Newton remained celibate. I wonder are most Catholic priests geniuses? I wonder are there any female geniuses?"

John cleared his throat. "I wonder... are there any... female...Catholic priests?"

"I wonder why aren't there any female Catholic priests, John?"

"Ask your good friend,... the universe!"

"All it'll do is answer my question with a question." I paused then: "But it did tell me that...at the present time, creative talent of priesthood isn't widely bestowed on women."

John cocked his head. "Ask it to... please repeat that."

Again, I paused. Then: "It said that the Virgin Mary bestows greatness on all women of the world just as The Lord Jesus bestows greatness on all men."

He shrugged and scratched his forehead.

Then, thinking about O.J., I said, "And listen to this, John! It also said that folks who possess creative talent are oftentimes regarded with awe and envy because they have this gift. Perhaps that's why folks envied Jesus and crucified him. Others regarded him with awe. And two thousand years after his death, most of the world still regard him with awe."

"He's our... example of... greatness."

"Genius is greatness; but folks who are geniuses are often thought of as peculiar; odd people who don't share the feelings of pains and suffering like other folks."

"I don't... go along with that,.. Alice."

"Neither do I. Because the gifts that enable people to become great writers and thinkers like Immanuel Kant are usually set in motion because of a happiness they've lost or because they were isolated. Three of Kant's siblings died in infancy, his mother died when he was thirteen and his father died when he was twenty-two. Kant developed cerebral arteriosclerosis, he was plagued with nightmares."

"But he was a great... philosopher."

Nodding, I pointed to John's forehead. "I like his theory that the *mind* is actively involved in the objects it experiences. It blends in with my belief that the mind is thoughts and feelings. God is mind. I learned that in solitude."

"Solitude's ...a human need, Alice."

"I've learned that it is. Dr. Kensinger said that the capacity to be alone enhances self-discovery and self-realization. It's linked with becoming aware of one's deepest needs and one's thoughts and feelings."

"In moderation."

"I'm keeping everything in balance."

"It's a thin line.. between.. balance... and imbalance."

"I'm not flirting with the edges, but I do love that upper room."

"We all do. It's home."

When he said "We all do; it's home" I could hear my heart pounding with fear. I squeezed my eyes and lowered my head, praying that I was not reading too much into his last statement.

I snapped out of my moment of depression and began running away from the graveyard as fast as my mind could carry me, taking John along with me on the literary journey. I thought about O.J. playing golf as a mind/body medicine.

We talked about my playmother and how I wanted to write about her and found it to be too much like the present situation. We talked about Simpson's case, his mind/body medicine of playing golf, the importance of understanding our true nature, and learning how to live in harmony with natural law in order to have a sense of well-being, energy and enthusiasm for life. We talked about how politics dominated the Simpson case.

"I told you the case is getting more and more educational with the books being written by the lawyers!" he said, laughing heartily even as Nurse DuVal entered to give him his usual insulin shot and tell us that the verdict was ready.

"The verdict's in!" I shrieked. Then kissing my husband on the forehead, I snatched my purse from the nightstand and hurried from hospital room enroute home. Weaving through bumper-to-bumper traffic like millions of curious Americans, my mind was anxious to hear President Clinton's speech and anxious to take a guilty peep at the verdict in theTrial of the Century. It was approximately six-thirty in the evening when I reached home. All the way home I thought about how the defense lawyer for Goldman had painted Simpson as a killer and, like most African Americans, I had a very difficult time believing this, too, but not beyond a reasonable doubt.

After arriving home, I felt exhausted, confused, and guilty in my agony to make choices.

Ironically, I relaxed in the Florida room with its white furniture and its ceiling-to-floor mirrors and white curtains, not to mention the white tiled floor, to watch the White jury seal a Black celebrity's fate.

Feeling overly stressed-out, yet disturbed about my anger and confusion, I meditated for one hour, asking for a quiet conscience and that I continue to make myself useful. Now relaxed, I was ready to enjoy the media's educational presentations on the TV screen, my once nervous hand punching out of control the remote control. Sure I wanted to hear every word of President Clinton's speech but the news media kept intercepting with sensational comments regarding the civil trial. I felt grateful but guilty. Realizing my anxiety, I pleaded for the Creator to calm over my being with a message of love and service.

My higher consciousness kept telling me that the message was universal and that I needed to listen attentively in order to help create a society of laws, principles, philosophy and morality to elevate humanity above its coarsest emotional impulses of anger, vengeance, retribution and killing to solve a problem.

CHAPTER SIX

Lord, when doubts fill my mind, when my heart is in turmoil, quiet me and give me renewed hope and cheer.
Psalm 94:19

The State of the Union message was on target! Why? Because the media with its genius reporting had locked our attention in a Shakespearean tragedy and now we wanted out, but not at the expense of moving backwards. Like a drug addiction, some of us needed help from a higher source...an amazing grace... because, spiritually, we were being blinded and lost by racism. This case was dividing our country and we were receiving a very disturbing message.

The verdicts were unanimous: Mr. Simpson was liable on all eight counts and was ordered to compensate the parents of Mr. Ron Goldman with the sum of $8.5 million for his wrongful death. Most Whites cheered.

I folded in tears. For deep within my heart all I could see was the innocent little three-year-old with rickets wearing his homemade braces with bar which his mother made and who, with the Grace of his Creator, rose to celebrity status and was loved by all humanity. What happened? Domestic violence is an evil behavior that shatters the continuity of the family, that destroys healthy relationships, individuals and spirituality! **Mother Nature Never Forgives**!

But all I also saw were two little babies, Nicole and Ron.

Even though my mind quietly told me to use my therapy in

understanding and dealing with the excruciating pain, I was still folded in tears. With anxiety, I switched to Channel 10.

And then a strange and intellectual thing happened. The verdict prompted President Clinton to call on America to respect the verdict and move on.

When he made that statement, I jumped to my feet, applauding! I felt as though a load was lifted from my heart. With renewed strength and a new beginning, I did move on, listening to The State of the Union Speech to keep my faith in America and its judicial system. In his speech that advocated meaningful solutions to the country's real problems, President Clinton promised to mount a "Crusade for Education." His speech focused on the country's future, education needs, moral and aesthetic values for our children, and the country's deficit reduction.

"Education!" I repeated, again jumping from the recliner and applauding. "The more intelligent, the less prejudice because what goes into the mind comes out in life! Man is the being by which values exist. As educators, we all know that America can save itself only as all children are lifted!"

President Clinton pointed to our need to build character in our children.

I listened because he had messages for our suffering, multicultural society. In the State of the Union Speech, when the president said that "our multiculturalness is our strength!" both my arms shot up in midair and I bounced from the recliner and did the Twist about the room repeating his statement.

Seconds later, I curled up in the recliner and continued listening attentively. I listened because our children are our future...our hope for a world of social justice, universal peace and brotherly love!

I listened, grateful for the president's dynamic leadership on the night when it seemed Americans were more concerned with Simpson's punitive financial state than the deteriorated spiritual and financial state of the union.

Following the intellectual speech, I said,"Thank you, Mr. President, for drying our tears! The business of education is to perfect human nature, and heaven knows we Americans are thirsty for multicultural education, especially following the Simpson case!"

I stared into the screen, still applauding the speech that restored my soul and renewed my faith in beautiful America and all humanity!

"Education is the key to perfect humanity!" I rapped, clasping my palms and doing a liturgical dance, weaving around and about leather furniture in praise to the universe for giving us godly leaders to match our mountains.

Then, curling up in the recliner, I listened to soul brother Republican Representative Watts' reply to the address, then began switching stations to see who was feeling the frustrations I was feeling concerning the shocking verdict prior to President Clinton's State of the Union completed and awakening speech. I was eager to hear what the lay people and the news reporters were saying in spite of the applauding seen on the screen by those who seemed bent on punishment, not justice. The verdict, to me, would add fuel to racial tensions unless we all acceded to the president's request to accept the jury's verdict and move on. Although to most of us African Americans, the amount was outrageous!

To hear the Whites say that the civil jury was doing its job the way the criminal jury should have done its made me feel very uncomfortable. Angered by this accusation, I flipped off the TV, then turned it on again because I was very thirsty for an explanation. Mr. Petrocelli, Mr. Goldman's defense lawyer, did a great job, and was true to his profession; and so did Simpson's defense lawyers in the criminal case. Carefully examining this, I now understood the difference between "reasonable doubt" and "preponderance of evidence."

According to voices heard over the radio stations, some callers were angry because it seemed the media made the Simpson verdict priority over the president's State of the Union speech...a president who was trying to stop violence. Some callers felt that O.J. was guilty but the penalty was far out of range. Some felt "Mr. Simpson was unjustly tried, wrongfully found liable, and penalized for a crime he didn't commit." Another caller felt that the case spelled the eventual lost of the principles proclaimed by the founders of America. Some callers felt that the civil case seemed to foreshadow a coming social, political and economic revolution; others called the civil trial a Kangaroo court; some called it a 21st Century style lynching. Several callers expressed their gratitude that it was all over, and some blamed the media for the "the dumbing of America."

The following Friday thousands of cheering, multicultural school children enjoyed seeing the life of Ella Fitzgerald: The Lady and Her Music, in celebration of Black History Month. John and I were ecstatic. This was mind/body medicine for Miami.

One week following the civil jury's guilty verdict, the jury assessed the punitive damages against Mr.Simpson in favor of both plaintiffs, Mr. Goldman and Mr. Brown. The verdict was almost unanimous. Simpson was ordered to pay $25 million more in damages. The following day most headliners read: *O.J. hit for $25 million more* in damages. We were shocked!

According to research, the polling of the jury voted yes and the vote was 11-2 to the question: Shall punitive damages be assessed against defendant Orenthal James Simpson in favor of plaintiff Fredric Goldman? In a 11-2 vote, the jury assessed $12.5 punitive damages against Mr.Simpson in favor of Mr. Goldman for loss of their son's love and companionship. In response to the third question, the jury voted yes, 11-1 that punitive damages be assessed against defendant Orenthal James Simpson in favor of plaintiff Louis Brown. With a vote of 10-2, the jury assessed $12.5 million in punitive damages against Mr. Simpson in favor of Mr. Brown for the estate of Nicole Brown Simpson whose beneficiaries include her two children now living with their father, Mr. Simpson. In the days that followed, O.J. Simpson's name became synonymous with the racial divide in America. But to me, it was also synonymous with domestic violence.

Why was I obsessed with the case? As a neophyte in all the matters of law, I was anxious to siege the opportunity of being taught through observation the strengths and weaknesses of our legal system (i.e., the safeguards built in to protect the accused if one has money to avail himself to all the safeguards). Every discipline has its own vocabulary. We observed, listened and learned something about motions, leading questions, admissibility, relevance and other figures of speech. Yes, we listened, we learned, we responded, using our multiculturalness as our strength in respecting each other's views with wisdom.

According to research, we Americans responded to the presence of TV cameras in the courtroom with affirmation because of the educational value of seeing the proceedings ourselves. There were a few who thought that having TV cameras in the courtroom during the criminal trial pushed the lawyers and judge to ridiculous extremes of "nitpicking and redundancy." Perhaps this was true in part, but being on camera was certainly instrumental in prompting them to rise to their highest professional levels of performance, especially our Mrs. Marcia Clark, prosecutor in a White male dominated society. Am I prejudiced? Yes, because Simone DeBeauvoir, in her book *The Second Sex*, said that to gain the supreme victory it is necessary that, by and through their natural differentiation, men and women unequivocally affirm their brotherhood. But, and this is very frightening, some of us Blacks and Whites who weren't listening carefully enough also learned "the disturbing message that justice is in the color of the beholder."

When I read this quote from the February 17, 1997 issue of *Time Magazine* as stated by Mr.Christopher Darden, a prosecutor in the Simpson criminal trial and an African-American, I applauded. Indeed, man is the being by which values exist.

From the very first linking of Mr. Simpson to the murders, Afro-American and White America went "bipolar" (bipolar means having two poles). They stayed that way throughout the trials with approximately two-thirds of Whites certain Mr. Simpson was guilty of the murders and two-thirds of us African-Americans doubting that Mr. Simpson was guilty of the murders but he was definitely guilty of wife abuse. We felt that he was framed by policemen with a history of brutality toward Blacks. Many who felt Mr. Simpson was innocent of the murders believed that racists policemen planted the evidence with their built-in mechanism to keep Black men under control...to kill them, if possible to jail them for lengthy periods or to break them financially.

Naturally Whites thought Mr. Simpson's acquittal was a miscarriage of justice, and African-Americans thought the civil trial (i.e., a private suit for money damages) was the "system's" attempt to find him guilty and punish him regardless.

One news commentator said that what we saw may have been racial only "in the sense that Black people, based on bitter experiences, are less likely than White people to assume the disinterested veracity of White policemen." This difference in experiences does not actually make us a divided people. What makes us nervous is that "in the criminal trial, it was a mixed jury that returned the not-guilty verdict. In the civil case, there were no Blacks on the jury that returned the guilty verdict and the massive award of $33.5 million." Some African-Americans feel that the cases demonstrate how the mental state of racism serves to impair the ability to reason in its otherwise intelligent victims.

Two weeks following the civil verdict, I sat in my office reading *The Miami Times*. My eyes were drawn to a letter written to the editor. The heading read: "Justice was not served in the O.J. Farce." Silently, I read:

To the editor:

By choosing a scapegoat and rushing to judgment which was the ceremonial dressing before sending the goat into oblivion, the LAPD and the media made a mockery of justice in America. Moreover, the real perpetrators in the Simpson/Goldman murders were given license to kill again as racial America gloated over the so-called vindication for the loss of two human beings.

For many Americans, the double jeopardy trial was no vindication at all. The quest for money overtook the search for the truth. The double jeopardy verdict only enhances the vacuum of hunger and thirst for justice and righteousness in the consciousness of America; it does not and cannot appease the demand for justice.

Of course, those whose psyche is chafed by the lifestyle of O.J. Simpson might have sensed some measure of appeasement in the second verdict and those who seek to benefit financially from this horrendous deed might also sense a measure of appeasement. But do they sense that justice was served?

The victims, the suspect, the families of the victims and the people were all short-changed of justice in the Simpson Saga. As the court seeks ways and means to bleed the estate of the scapegoat, it will become evident that the love of money is at the root of this terrible farce played on the public.

The LAPD never took into consideration the racial climate in America, which is very real; it colors and influences all that we do on a societal level, how we interact and respond to each other. The racial climate cannot be brushed aside; it must be reckoned with. The old-attic racial ideas of yesteryear which were breast-fed and spoon-fed to America's youth are bringing fourth fruits today in most of the civic institutions in the land; the disparate treatment which it fosters is still there.

As subtle as the criminal justice system tried to make it in the Simpson Saga, the disparate treatment only added intrigue to the tragedy.

Nor did the LAPD take into consideration the golfers...those who attach themselves to the rich and famous for a free ride in exchange for a long range of services (you name it). Many of these bring with their services, heavy baggage and are closely connected with the merchants of misery in our society. They know where the money veins are and, once they tap into them, will do anything to keep the flow going. The LAPD might have not seriously considered the golfers but the media gave them enough coverage to sensationalize tragedy.

The media is most valuable in a free and open society such as ours but, often, it facilitates the suppression of the truth in exchange for sensationalism...or to keep from offending certain segments of society.

- Veola B. Williams, Miami

Ironically, during this same period in which viewers were attacking the media for sensationalizing tragedy amid the calm and the strife, a mysterious coincidence occurred. The media's talk show hostess Oprah Winfrey was discussing with her viewers the importance of having a positive attitude, the joy of giving and the joy of expressing gratitude. With her keen insight, she suggested that we viewers begin keeping a daily journal on the many experiences for which we are grateful. In her messages, she was implying that gratitude is the basis for human happiness, and that gratitude is the memory of the heart.

Suddenly, it flashed before me that Oprah's insight was leading me into the era of true spiritual awareness. Writing in a daily journal about experiences for which we are grateful, was indeed the guidance we all needed at this point in history.

With this insight, my literary wings were ready to fly, especially inasmuch as my husband was excellent at suggesting the spiritual plots for our writings which we had been using as a form of therapy to ease the pain.

Based on life's universal teachings, I had learned from the trials that ingratitude is at the root of domestic violence and racism.

CHAPTER SEVEN

Writing is a form of therapy; sometimes I wonder how all those who do not write, compose or paint can manage to escape the madness, the melancholia, the panic fear which is inherent in the human situation.
Graham Green

Although racism entered the picture, we were not distracted because we saw the brighter picture The criminal and civil trials had awakened many of us concerned listeners to a new kind of self awareness as a people united, and we felt that the cases were uniting us in our Christ The King Catholic Church "Where love is international."

'We don't begin to live when we have solved our problems, we solve our problems by living," I recalled Father Dionne saying to me one morning following mass. I was questioning him about the lessons of *Genesis* and all the problems we humans inherited.

It was late February 1997 and I was again at my computer eager to complete Patty's story projecting domestic abuse and its evils. The experiences of both trials had awakened me to the seriousness that domestic violence is a sin against the human person and a major societal problem that needs priority attention. The Case of the Century brought to our full attention that the world at times is filled with hostility and is racially divided; and that some people consider themselves dominant over others based on gender, race, color, class or status. The walls of hostility needed to be torn down for the intention of eliminating domestic violence against women and children..

Having researched abusive behaviors such as physical violence, sexual abuse, psychological abuse in which a person attempts to control the thinking, behavior or feeling of another, I was eager to write. I would speak to the subject of verbal abuse, its persistent name calling, degrading judgmental statements, yelling, etc. In writing about emotional abuse, I would highlight such subjects as deliberate acts of infidelity, minimizing, lying that destroys integrity and trust. Because some abusers have the habit of saying such phrases as: "I'll teach her a lesson;" I'll put her in her place" and "I'm gonna waste her" or "I'm gonna do the O. J. on you!" etc., I would speak to this kind of hostility by control freaks. I would speak on the issue of stalking, a subject of which I am very familiar. Stalking would involve any deliberate, calculated and persistent behavior intended to violate an individual's right to privacy and freedom of movement. In my experiences, these actions are directed toward the partner without their initial knowledge and continued despite specific request to stop once such actions are discovered. Stalking is an abusive kind of behavior which I perceived as intimidating, frightening, threatening and emotional terrorism.

Yes, the criminal and civil trials were educational in that they awakened us to the awareness that domestic violence against women leaves them abused and battered, oppressed and broken, minimized, ridiculed, threatened, violated, excluded, harassed, ignored, raped, exploited, discriminated against, passed over, invisible, undervalued and all the ills that destroy a woman's healthy physical, social and psychological development.

I typed far into the afternoon, thumbing through research I had gathered for the book and was touched by a prayer I had found among the files. Placing it in my black briefcase along with *The Miami Times* and copies of *Time* magazine, I hurried to Coral Reef Library to work on further research the librarian had put aside for me.

Dee met me at the library to offer assistance as usual. We sat in a quiet room opposite the auditorium, working attentively and sharing a wealth of knowledge we had learned about the controversial case that would give added momentum to our research.

We talked about violence. We talked painfully about the senseless shooting death of Bill Cosby's 27-year old only son, Ennis, who graduated from Morehouse, the same college from which my husband graduated. The whole world was shaken by Ennis' death as though America had suffered a painful death in its own beloved family because everyone loved Bill Cosby, an outstanding television father. Young Ennis had driven off the Los Angeles freeway to change a flat tire when a robber approached and shot him. Young, handsome and intelligent, Ennis was a doctoral student and taught children with learning disabilities.

"Violence," Dee said, and spoke about racial hate letters Black students at Coral Gables and Miami Beach High found in their lockers this week. "Young White racists are watching Los Angeles. What are we teaching our children?"

"The wrong message," I said dismally. "Now that the verdict is in, I hope the world doesn't push violence on the back burner again."

"I'm afraid they will, unless O.J. decides to be a voice as a tribute to his deceased wife. Simpson generates huge audiences and money if Americans can get past the race card again like we were prior to the tragedy. His ability to draw world attention and generate millions of dollars is a gift from his Creator."

"Well, Dee, lots of people are still disturbed about the verdicts. And the most noble thing we can do now for the victims is to launch a massive program to help stop domestic violence to help save the children."

Dee agreed. " When Mr. Darden was asked why did they lose the criminal trial and the plaintiffs won the civil trial he stated that it was simple: different judges, different jury, different lawyers, different evidence, different day."

I nodded, feeling the need to move on with our research. "Dee, I can understand how the juries in both trials reached their contradictory verdicts."

"How? Both Simpson's and Goldman's defense lawyers were great."

"According to the standard of criminal trials, the prosecutors didn't prove their case beyond a reasonable doubt. And because there was a lot of evidence against Simpson, that was all the civil trial needed to find him liable."

"And then too, Alice, the civil trial focused more tightly on Simpson instead of the police, especially Mr. Fuhrman and that taped-conversation. When O.J. denied having the infamous Bruno Magli shoes which the jury could see with their own eyes, and then saying he had never struck his wife was detrimental to the case. Actually, he was his own worst witness."

"He's very intelligent. I'm sure he knows it."

"O.J. has come to symbolize crime, race and justice."

"My focus is domestic abuse."

"Justice is lots of money," she said, shaking out the pages of *The Miami Times* which she pulled from my briefcase. Are you as confused about the case as I am?"

I nodded my "Yes" because I thought the deceased victims were short-changed of justice.

"Well, you're mighty quiet about this verdict. I don't get it."

"President Clinton called on America to respect the verdict and move on, Dee; and that's exactly what I'm trying to do. But I'm sure when we begin researching the various books and articles about it written by the professionals, we'll understand it better. And who knows, perhaps the universe will even put this Trial of the Century on the Internet."

Dee laughed softly. "You really believe that, don't you?"

"Dee, everyone, from the greatest genius to the most lowly beggar, reflects the beliefs and the living conditions of his own time."

"What does that suppose to mean?"

"The statement's self explanatory, Dee. Actually, this seems to be a universal law that can be seen in the Bible and in Shakespeare's writings that grasp the worldwide audiences."

"This whole case was like a Shakespeare drama, you once said."

Flipping through a folder entitled Domestic/Repeat Violence Injunction Information Sheets, I continued to explain. "And now we're in the age of modern technology...A technological evolution that 's the 'thinking envelope' of the Earth and which entails a kind of 'etherized universal consciousness' that'll finally lead us to an era of brotherly love which we'd been seeking before Adam and Eve bit off that apple."

" You and all this research about modern technology."

"Well, Dee, the universe has a way of teaching us all through suffering and pain. Through pain and suffering we learn how to create and solve problems."

"Speaking of problems, did you hear Oprah Winfrey reading all those angry letters people, both White and Black, wrote to her after she had Mark Fuhrman on her talk show?"

"I heard her reading them, and I heard some of the ones sent to Chris Darden from both White and Black people. I don't think people are aware of how much hatred they feel. They're kind of immune to it. That's why the Simpson case is actually our case, too. We can't afford to point fingers. 'He who is without fault, let his cast the first stone.'"

"I can now fully understand that. We've gotta continue to learn from each other and help each other evolve."

"That's the spirit, Dee! Life teaches us by example that the higher and more delicate the development of a human being, the more sensitive he becomes to suffering. And that true joy, on the other hand, has to be learned and practiced as a virtue, and it comes to us as a present from our Creator through grace, according to Fathers Dionne and Clements."

"My minister said that joy isn't a part of our existence, Alice, but our existence is completed with it, though. He said the source of true joy is found in suffering. I didn't know that. Of course you've always said that joy gains its glory out of suffering...bitter suffering and man's loneliness."

"We hurt when others hurt; we're happy when others are happy as long as they're not hurting someone else."

"I just felt very sad about all the people involved, especially the victims."

"That's the love in you, Dee."

"Well anyway, I'm sure that everyone's glad it's over with."

I laughed and shook my head. "With your experiences you should know by now that every fulfillment is only the fulfillment of a further search!"

"Oh no, Alice. I hope society's not gonna be searching for anything else that emotional!"

"My analyst said that we must always be ready for a new task and must have the courage to be discontented."

"Well, I'll tell you what,... you go right ahead with your courage to be discontented; and continue your massive research on domestic abuse. I've had more than enough of this Kangaroo Court. Lots of folks called it double jeopardy."

"My lawyer said it wasn't double jeopardy. He said the Supreme Court has long upheld trial for the same offense by separate jurisdictions. He said that a civil jury found Mr., Simpson culpable in the deaths of Nicole and Ron after he was acquitted of murder."

I understood what Dee was saying, but I was determine to fight this monster called domestic violence for the victims and the millions of other victims and wasn't about to let anything block me.

"Alice, have you had dinner?"

"When I'm locked into writing and research, I forget about eating."

"I'm talking about dinner, not snacking on brownies."

I knew that the library was no place for us to be carrying on conversations, so I agreed to go with her to Morrison's for dinner. When we arrived, we both ordered a seafood platter. The conversation turned to questions about our spiritual mission, where does it begin and where does it end? She wanted to know why did I consider it my mission to help stop the violence?

She shook out the pages of *The Miami Times* to continue reading. With reluctance, I answered her question, feeling that her mind was on whatever it was she was reading. "Dee, I've always been told that experience has a right to speak with authority. So, I considered it my mission because, unfortunately, I have the experience of being an abused spouse."

"Maybe the Master was preparing you for this mission."

"The only truths we know is that we do not know. Anyway, to share the experiences to help others kept gnawing at me. I felt restless and depressed every time I heard of someone being abused. And I felt extremely hostile toward the abuser but I buried the feelings of hostility because it wasn't Christlike to hate people. Experiences of childhood kept creeping into my thoughts and feelings but I'd ignore them. Finally, when the Trial of the Century exploded in the media, and I discovered that our worldwide hero whom the world loved and adored was a wife abuser, I was angry, frustrated, confused and depressed until my analyst suggested that I write out my frustrations. It seemed my world of experiences with domestic violence exploded along with feelings of stifled hate for the abusers. And then I had to deal with this buried hate that had come ashore with Jesus's 'Father, forgive them for they know not what they do.'"

Dee jerked her head from the paper and stared hard at me. "I'm sorry, Alice, I just don't buy that! No-o-o-o. Men who beat their wives know darn well what they're doing. They're not stupid, they're evil bastards!"

I chuckled. "Feeling like you didn't help me stop feeling hate for them. My parents told me when I was a child to hate the violence, not the person. You should never let anyone drag you so low as to make you hate them. That's the way I interpreted Jesus's prayer: 'Father, forgive them for they know not what they do.' So, I decided to use my therapy and examine the psychological foundations of domestic violence. Socrates believed that goodness in a man is based on wisdom, and wickedness is based on ignorance."

"O.J. is very intelligent and full of wisdom."

"That's why the pain of discovering that he abused his wife was cutting so deeply into our hearts. Being an abusive spouse just didn't fit his dynamic personality."

"It was shocking," she said as the waitress brought our attractive seafood platters.

While we were eating, we launched into a discussion about Simpson's bestseller entitled *I Want To Tell You*, sharing our experiences on how much we enjoyed reading it.

"But, Dee, it still pains me that he was abusive, especially when we women strongly believe that each individual is a valuable human being who is entitled to a healthy physical, social and psychological development."

"How do you plan to help the cause, Alice?" She sipped from her coffee. "You're gonna ask your sorority sisters Representatives Meek and Bullard, and nurses like Marie Mohammed?"

"Yes. I'm gonna work with the National Council of Catholic Women. As a member, we have a program in which we educate both men and women on the issue of domestic violence. We're gonna address this issue by offering support in word and action to women and families who are victims of abuse. We're gonna advocate for legislation that address the issue of domestic violence. You see, Dee, one of our church members is a Florida Senator and his wife is on my board of church commissions."

"Who? Senator Darryl Jones' wife, Myoshia?"

I nodded. "She chairs our Legislation Commission at Christ

the King. We're also gonna see can we rally the nation against gangsta rappers and get these big companies to stop selling music that glorifies violence. Gangsta music is shocking and provocative! It revels in the degradation of women; it revels in violence and vulgarity, in drugs, crassness, loutish behavior and every act that promotes the epitome of violence."

"Yes, Alice, but these big companies get big money for that brand of rap music. We're almost powerless. "

"That's why we as responsible adults have gotta show our disapproval by their censure, not censorship. It's destroying our young people and sending them the wrong message that violence is a balm, a tranquilizer.

"I see no reason why you can't let all the commission heads do something in the area of assisting battered women and children.

"All Council affiliates are involved. The president of the South Dade Deanary, Pat Howard, is a member of Christ the King. She's dynamic and so are the members of the Women's Guild!"

Dee applauded. "So, you're joining a host of hard working Catholic women who are already dealing with the issue."

"Yes. They're also working to make funding of shelters and educational programs for battered women and children a federal priority."

"With a disabled husband, what makes you think you can do all this?" Dee asked, cutting into her baked salmon. She talked about how she hardly has time to do community work because of her teaching position...although she would love to work with at-risk youth.

I listened, then shared with her some things I had learned from our priests. "Indirectly, Father Haynes and those have led us to understand that the full measure of our being is boundlessness, and yet this longing must always remain enclosed within the smallness of what can be reached on earth."

"That's understandable."

" According to their counseling, achieving a Christlike

personality is a lifetime task which is never completed. They explained that it's a journey upon which one sets out hopefully toward a destination at which one never arrives."

Somewhere in the conversation, when I told her that the flow of life again and again demands fresh adaptation, and that adaptation is never achieved once and for all, she laughed and suggested we change the conversation.

I laughed, too. "Even changing the conversation is fresh adaptation."

We did change our conversation and began talking about finding God in the Web and how believers are re-examining their ideas of faith, religion and spirituality across the Internet. We talked throughout dinner.

" Researchers feel that the Internet is God's will," I said, as the shapely, friendly waitress removed our plates.

"Desserts?" the waitress smiled and asked. Dee and I smiled and said "No Thanks" simultaneously.

"Why are we into all this technology, Alice?" Dee asked, then sipped from her cup of decaf coffee and began reading *The Miami Times*. "For some reason, I'm still concerned about those trials."

"Perhaps you're suffering from post O.J. stress disorder like most of us. That's why I'm anxious to write, praying that I don't get writer's block again."

" Speaking of writers, here's some good research for you," she said, pointing to an article in the *Miami Times* and handing the newspaper to me, "Lots of people are as confused as you, Alice. Read what Viola Williams of Miami had to say. She's another woman who feels that justice wasn't served in the O.J. Simpson farce. It's a letter to the editor."

"I've read it."

She implied that Folks said the bottom line was "The Almighty" dollar and that justice had nothing to do with it.

The following day while visiting John at VA, we talked about the letter written to the editor of *The Miami Times* and about the book I was doing on Patty while I spoonfed him his prescriptioned-dinner. He had been up for over two hours and the nurses had placed him back in bed.

It amazed me how eager he was to express his concern for our research on domestic violence. He implied that it was good I had worked myself out of the writer's block, and that time operates the law of compensation, but it doesn't always do it swiftly.

"I want to write about the art of being human," I said, removing his dinner tray and slightly lowering the head of his bed.

"Wouldn't that come under the subject?" he asked, pointing to his eyeglasses that were on the food tray.

Handing him the glasses, I replied, "Sweetheart, I'm finding a lot of good research and am over anxious to finish the book."

Before dinner, we had been reading the February 3, 1997 issue of *Time* magazine. Especially interesting was a special report on how a child's brain develops, and what it means for child care and welfare reform. The colorful center-page of the magazine spoke to its headline: *Is O.J. Really Broke?*

I showed my husband the article, then cleaned his eyeglasses and placed them on his eyes. "Do you still feel angry that he abused his wife?"

My eyes widened. "Come to think of it, John, I do feel angry! I feel very angry. I feel angry with myself for not having the guts to speak out against violence of any kind because I'm too blind to see its roots. All violent behavior usually begins in childhood and stems from a violent home environment!"

"We know this."

"Certainly!" I said, pointing to the cover of *Time* magazine that portrayed the face of a beautiful, healthy baby, highlighting those innocent eyes of its world. The portrait displayed the child's forehead (brain) with pictures of children (perhaps his own) experiencing life's activities.

Seeing this and sharing it with my husband, I said, "Certainly we know that violence begins in childhood. And mothers can help shape the experiences of their infants. All MEN are born of WOMEN! Some men grow up to be abusive. That's why we abused women have gotta stop sweeping domestic violence under the rug because we're ashamed to let our neighbors and friends know that we're being battered by this husband who is suppose to love us! "

"Oh boy."

"We concerned women have gotta help save our generations of young children! Women are the ones who give birth to these precious, innocent babies, therefore the pregnant mother could start teaching her unborn child the principles of love and nonviolence while it's yet in the womb. And by the time that child is three years old, he and his generation is prepared to begin building a world of non-violent men."

"What if he sees his daddy beating his mother during those formative years, Alice? "

Silence. I thought about a childhood experience my husband once shared with me about how he saw his sixteen-year-old uncle beating his eighteen-year-old mother and he wanted to kill him.

Ironically, John broke the silence with: "When I was a student at old Woodward in Cincinnati, I remembered one of my classmates beating the dickens outta his drunk father for always beating on his mother when he was a child. He kept that anger in his heart a long time, until he was big enough to do something about it."

"That often happens and is swept under the rug when the man is the basic breadwinner, sweetheart. And many husbands have a fat billfolder and the woman is afraid to leave because no one wants to live in poverty."

"Write that down."

I told him that I did. The research was in my unfinished novel, *Kennetta*, which he once angrily ripped up and dumped in the garbage can when his multiple sclerosis came aboard and tried to turn him into a wife abuser.

"Oh boy!" he said and kneaded his forehead. "I'm sorry."

I squeezed his hand and continued. "But I understood and I loved you. At least we learned that it was our mysterious stranger aboard and not you."

"That monster," he joked of his mysterious illness for which there is still no cure.

I laughed and said to my John. "Maybe it's good we didn't have any kids. Remember when that registered nurse came home to her handsome husband who had MS and her two beautiful children and blew their brains out because she was frustrated and confused?"

John nodded his head. "She and my mother were the best of friends and we could not believe a kind, beautiful lady like her would do a thing like that."

I nodded. "She didn't deny doing it. The judge understood that she was under tremendous stress and she was acquitted. Not because she was White, but because those who knew her well, told the judge that she was overly stressed to the point of almost losing her mind. They said he abused her!"

"She should have left."

"You know what, John? As a caregiver myself, I was wondering why didn't she just leave like many other spouses whose better halves have MS and they find it too stressful. Perhaps that's why they leave, to avoid being violent abusers or being violently abused."

"Do some research on that."

"I think I will; especially with spouses where children are involved."

"Maybe they do it to save the children."

I agreed. "Our present generation of children are growing up battering and killing each other because they see their grown-up fathers beating up their mothers! 'Stop the tide of violence!' the Dade County School Board member, Frederica Wilson, is pleading. She's the founder of 'Stop Day' the state's having on the last Thursday in March, this month. The aim is to end attacks among schoolchildren; to make anti-violence the new cause among students. It's statewide and students throughout Florida will pause and meditate on a year of violence that's affected children. There'll also be speakers and other projects."

"Oh boy! Keepers of the dream!"

"Yes, they're keeping King's dream of non-violence alive." I thought about how a woman carrying her baby and how a little five-year-old girl walking home from our 1997 Martin Luther King Day Parade were both killed by stray bullets. I thought about *The Miami Times* recent article on Kim and Lucy, two high school students here in Miami who were good friends. The article spoke of how Lucy, in a confrontation and a fit of anger, pulled a gun from her backpack and shot Kim in the eye and when Kim slumped to the ground, unconscious, Lucy angrily stood over her, kicking her several times and still furiously arguing. The papers implied that it is very difficult to reach our children who are already hardened by violence. I thought about violence on TV.

Nodding my head, I stared at John and said: "Honey, I was deeply moved by a statement Mrs. Wilson made about violence. She said: 'It's horrifying, the mentality of the children. We have to be forever vigilant. We can't rest. We can't sleep. These are our children that we're losing to this mindset, this violence!' Mrs. Wilson has always spoken up for the children who're caught up in a world of stress that's causing a lot of violence."

John nodded. "I agree, Alice. We've all gotta help save the children."

"Gotta keep writing docudramas about positive role models who devote their lives to help suffering humanity on this spiritual journey."

I thought about my belated friend, Sally, who said Simpson, after becoming a hero, was not a victim of racism but he helped suffering humanity. My mind flashed back on an article I had read. It stated that we fail to realize that football players like O.J. serve to reduce stress by diverting the attention of both the White and Black masses. It further stated that intoxicated by alcohol and high on drugs, the American working class blows off steam and reduces stress by watching the Packers and the Patriots, figuratively and literally, destroy each other. The masses enjoyed watching O.J. play football. They loved him!

I also thought about Simpson's life as an outstanding athlete and his Trial of the Century that should go down in history for a number of reasons (ex: celebrity and racism). James Baldwin, one of the most prolific Black writers of modern times consistently treated racism as a disease of White society throughout his literary works. He was a playwright, essayist, and novelist who received a host of honors for literary triumphs. These honors included a Guggenheim Literary Fellowship, a Ford Foundation grant-in-aid, a Partisan Review Fellowship and a National Institute of Arts and Letters Award in 1956. In adulthood, he achieved his childhood dream of being an honest man and a good writer.

John tugged at his eyeglasses "Yeah, Alice, let's write to help save the little ones." He took *Time* magazine and began reading the article about the minds of babies. The article stated that the first three years of the baby's life are critical. It further stated that a baby's brain cells proliferate wildly from birth, making connections that may shape a lifetime of experiences.

After adjusting his bed covers, I began watering the philodendron plants in the white duck planters on the nightstands. My mind drifted into deep thought as I moved into the hallway, watering the myriad of green plants that adorned the nursing station's long counter.

One of the joys of growing older in years is having faith in the fundamental capacity to dream and create, I silently said to the universe. All great changes and reforms come about because someone exercised the questioning and the kind of curiosity that stimulates growth...growth that has brought us to the age of technology in which we feel that the Internet is God's will. It will bring spiritual and moral values into the home. Hopefully it would help children to understand how to love their neighbors.

When I finished talking with the universe and returned to John's bedside, I thanked him for "bugging" me about finishing the book on domestic violence. Already, I felt overly excited about the opportunity to help save our generation of young people who would be our leaders of tomorrow.

We talked about writing children's books based on our musical docudramas that had been written and produced. We talked about "writing therapy" that would help children look into the depths of their souls and create on paper what's hurting inside.

And all the while we felt grateful to the universe for the spiritual, though painful, lessons we learned from both trials. But spiritual growth is painful.

My therapist has always implied that thoughts arise in company and their development and expression take place in solitude. I wanted to think in solitude. He had said that good books and conversation promote thoughts more than years of solitary toil; and perhaps that was why I enjoyed talking with my scholarly husband and my many friends, like Dee, and sharing good books read. I enjoyed the news media because it educates. In elementary school, we were taught how to read through the propaganda and brainwashing. We were taught that a person who loves to read good books can educate himself. Being an avid reader, a skill I learned in the first grade, I was interested in reading many of the books about the Trial of the Century written by various authors because of their educational values inasmuch as it has been said that every experience is a spiritual education. Life has taught us that human destiny makes us all brothers; we do not travel this journey alone. We have good reason to always be seriously concerned about the good or evil deeds we send into the lives of others; for these deeds...good and evil... come back into our own lives because, in her law of cause/effect, Mother Nature never forgives.

One hour after arriving home, I hurried to my quiet room and began meditating. With calmness of spirit, I asked to free myself from all stress, from all attachments; to eliminate delus*ions*, perverted views of the happenings in daily life; bad thinking habits of worrying about John's MS and racial tensions. I asked to be clear and tranquil as the early March stream that curved through the trenches of Coral Reef Park; and for compassion and clarity; to be humble so that a light could shine through me upon things and make me aware that I am nothing, but the light is all.

Trusting my own mind has always been essential to writing because words come out of the mind. I meditated: "O Creator, our world at times is divided and hostile. But please help us to continue this spiritual journey... to help stop domestic violence because it is a sin against the human person and a major societal problem which cuts across all racial, religious, ethnic, and socioeconomic boundaries in an abuse of women and children."

Life had taught me the great value of prayerful solitude, and that when we converse with the Creator, our understanding of life is deepened and our outlook is broadened. Talking with the Creator raises our thoughts and feelings above the narrow limits of our mortal existence. It is the highest height of joy!

Hours later and locked into my literary world, I was now enthusiastically motivated to keep my hands moving, to lose control, to be specific and to stay focused. I wanted to write hard and clear about what was hurting because it had all the energy to help create a world where love finds expression through kindness and concern admid the calm and the strife...

"Where cross the crowded ways of life
Where sound the cries of race and clan
Above the noise of selfish strife
We hear Thy voice, O Son of Man."

2

"Speak, Lord, for thy servant heareth." - 1 Sam. 3:9.

...Yes, we hear thy voice, O son of man, because in quietness, we are listening.

For the past six months I had been locked into my literary world of gratitude journal writing, and due to pensive listening, had already completed three books: *Let your Attitude Be Gratitude*, *Symbols of Love* and *A Journal for Caregivers*. Ironically, I was working on an unfinished manuscript entitled *Love Finds Expression Through Kindness and Concern* when I abruptly stopped to listen to the shocking newscasts on Sunday, August 31, 1997. Tears came quickly, streaming down my face.

The reports stated that Britain's Princess Diana had been killed earlier that morning along with her 42-year old companion, department store heir and movie executive Dodi Fayed, when their car crashed in a tunnel in Paris.

According to French radio, their Mercedes was apparently being chased by a motorcycle carrying paparazzi—the commercial photographers who constantly tail Princess Diana (and other celebrities), when the accident happened shortly after midnight, on Sunday, August 31. Two hours later at a news conference, an anesthesiologist at the state-run Pitie Salpetriere Hospital, where the 36-year-old Princess of Wales was taken after being cut from the wreckage, announced that she died at 4 a.m, Paris time (10 p.m. Eastern Daylight Time) Saturday, after going into cardiac arrest brought on by multiple serious car injuries.

The Sunday morning final edition of *The Miami Herald* headlines read *DIANA DIES...Boyfriend, driver also killed in wreck.*

And then it seemed the whole world collapsed into mourning.

The news media stated that Princess Diana, whose storybook marriage ended in a bitter divorce that shook the royal family, was "the people's princess."

One announcer stated that Diana Spencer was the stuff of classic fairy tale and contemporary human tragedy. How so? Because she married the prince and she rode in a horse-drawn carriage and captivated a world that loved her. But, like many of us humans, she did not live happily ever after and she did not live long.

Fortunately, her short life made a tremendous difference that set a new standard for style, class and purpose. Following her troubled marriage and painful divorce, she embarked on a magical life of unique and historic celebrity. Yes, by the time of her violent and untimely death, she had evolved into the standard of style, class and purpose against which elegant and intellectual women throughout the world measured themselves. She was, indeed, a humanitarian of world-class stature admired by all races and nationalities.

Dressed with the effortless confidence of a supermodel, Diana established herself as an activist shaped for a purpose. Wisely using her status of wealth, position and celebrity, she fought for causes as disparate as AIDS prevention, even shaking the hand of an AIDS victim. She spoke up for the eradication of land mines that killed and/or maimed hundreds of innocent children and adults. She showed compassion for some of life's least appealing unfortunates, from lepers to drug abusers. Her love was expressed through kindness and concern.

Unlike many celebrities, she paid dearly for her wealth and position, dauntlessly confronting half a lifetime of anguish and betrayal. She hid her pain until hiding became impossible. Sadly, we abused women identified with her suffering when biographer Andrew Morton wrote *Diana: Her True Story*. The book spoke of Diana's bouts with Bulimia, and that she had attempted suicide five times by the time her second son was born in 1984. Fans called her a humble, vulnerable, confused and mistreated, tender and loving young mother determined to salvage her dignity and do the correct thing for her loving children. After reading the book along with the hundreds of fairly and dispassionately recorded news articles (and, unfortunately, as well as the paparazzi) that followed, Diana's fans regarded her as the royal family's victim.

The London press implied that the royal family threw Diana out of the royal circle and took away her beloved title; but she still sparkled, undiminished, as the brightest gem in the House of Windsor crown.

To many of us women who have been abused, she was a sister in humiliation. Her feelings of depression resonated loudly with abused women of all social castes who know that domestic violence shatters the continuity of the family, and destroys healthy relationships, individuals and spirituality. We also know that psychological abuse is domestic violence, and that it is defined as any systematic attempt to control the thinking, behaviors or feelings of another. This includes the manipulation of the values and belief systems of the partner.

How did domestic abuse shatter the continuity of Diana's family?

Our religious counselors imply that the family is a number of individuals who come together with different past traditions, values, and attitudes, and share a common commitment, love and goals, growing towards a future united together with a living spirituality and faith. They counsel that domestic abuse shatters the continuity of the family. *"For I know well the plans I have in mind for you, says the Lord, plans for your welfare, not for woe. Plans to give you a future full of hope."*

Dauntless, young and brave, Diana, the princess of the people, did not let domestic abuse destroy her spiritual mission. In spite of her suffering, she moved toward her wildest dream of being a dynamic humanitarian who made a difference. Undoubtedly, she felt that her mission here on earth was to spread love. With courage, she took the labels off her mind and stepped boldly into her greatness, showing us by example that love is expressed through kindness and concern.

The spontaneous outpouring of love and sympathy from millions of people around the world along with mountains of flowers, cards and candles were seen and heard by us all as we mourned her death. She had begun to reinvent the role of the monarchy for the 21st Century. Indeed, this was her mission. She was the limelight of the royal family. She had set the standard for style, class, compassion and the new spiritual common sense as portrayed in *The Celestine Prophecy*, which is beginning to become the dominant paradigm of the 21st Century.

What is the spiritual message here? "We humans wanted too much and paid a horrible price," said writer Leonard Pits Jr., who, like most of us, is aware that paparazzi feed on the world's appetite for images of celebrities. We especially thirst for positive images of celebrities like Princess Diana, whose mystique captivated the public and presidents alike because she was a humanitarian of world-class stature. Amid the calm and the strife, we all are strengthen by her lifelong example of portraying social justice, universal peace and brotherly love. The spiritual message is clear.

> "*In haunts of wretchedness and need*
> *In shadowed thresholds dark with fears*
> *From paths where hide the lures of greed*
> *We catch the vision of thy tears*."

About The Authors

Alice W. Johnson, Ed. D., and John Johnson Jr., Ed.D., authors of *Mysterious Stranger Aboard*, *Love Paints Beauty in the Soul* and *The Calm and th* *Strife*, have spent most of their lives educatin youths and adults as teachers and through musica docudramas emphasizing multicultural education Their works, which portray the lives of outstandin role models who have triumphed over adversity have won them many awards and honors on th local, state and national levels.

Alice, a writer for *The Miami Times*, is a graduate c Savannah State University, Atlanta University an The University of Sarasota.

John, an educator, a U.S. Army Veteran and a victim of multipl sclerosis, is a graduate of Morehouse College, The University of Cincinnati an The University of Sarasota.

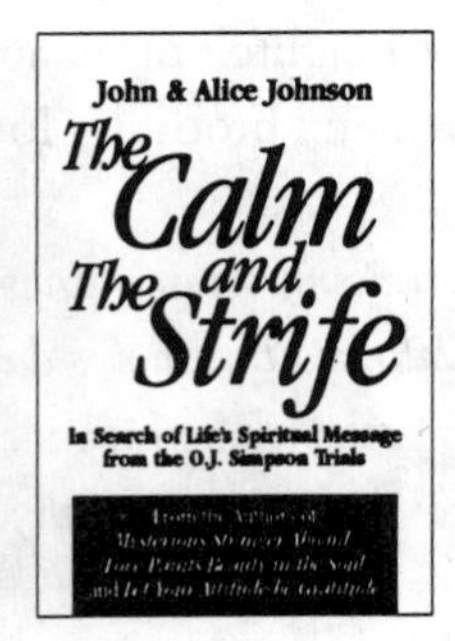

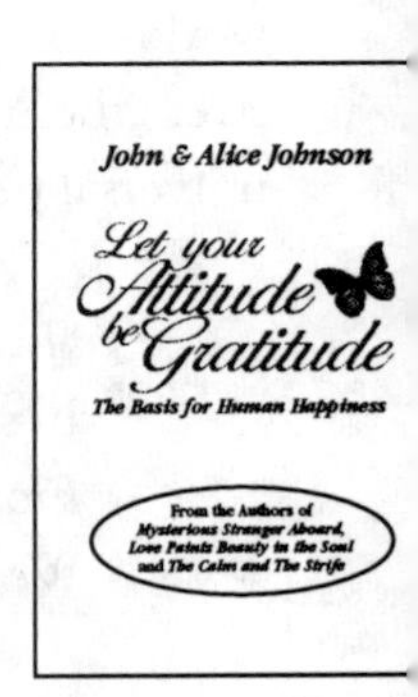

ORDER FORM

***Mysterious Stranger Aboard* - $10 ~ # of copies** _______

***Love Paints Beauty in the Soul* - $10 ~ # of copies** _______

***The Calm and The Strife* - $10 ~ # of copies** _______

***Let your Attitude be Gratitude* - $10 ~ # of copies** _______

$5 EACH FOR ORDERS OF 20 OR MORE!

Name ____

Address ______________________________________

City/State/Zip _________________________________

Phone Number ________________ **Fax Number** ________________

Make checks payable to Mal-Jonal Productions and mail to:

Mal-Jonal Productions, Inc.

16713 sw 107th Place

Miami, Florida 33157